SEVEN CHURCHES

GOD'S REVELATION
TO THE
CHURCH TODAY

MARSHALL NEAL

 Bob Jones University Press, Inc.
Greenville, South Carolina 29614

Seven Churches: God's Revelation to the Church Today

©1977 Bob Jones University Press, Inc.
Greenville, South Carolina 29614

ISBN: 0-89084-062-8

Printed in the United States of America

CONTENTS

PREFACE

Since the summer of 1969 I have been privileged to lead several study tours, sponsored by Bob Jones University, of the missionary journeys of Paul. In one month we visit as many of the places where Paul lived and worked and preached as possible, including the seven cities (in what is now Turkey) to whom the Book of Revelation is addressed. These trips sparked my interest in the Biblical background of the New Testament and in the historical as well as the homiletical aspects of the seven letters to the churches of Asia that form an introduction to the Book of Revelation. Since the first tour in 1969 I have read extensively on the background, history, and interpretation of this portion of Scripture. The results of this study are presented here.

I hope that this book will pass on to the reader something of the inspiration and blessing I have received while studying the seven churches and that it will move him to a new dedication to the cause of Christ, an increased interest in the study of the Word of God, and a desire to delve into the background of the New Testament for himself. Perhaps some will be motivated to visit this area and to study and see for themselves firsthand these fascinating Bible sites.

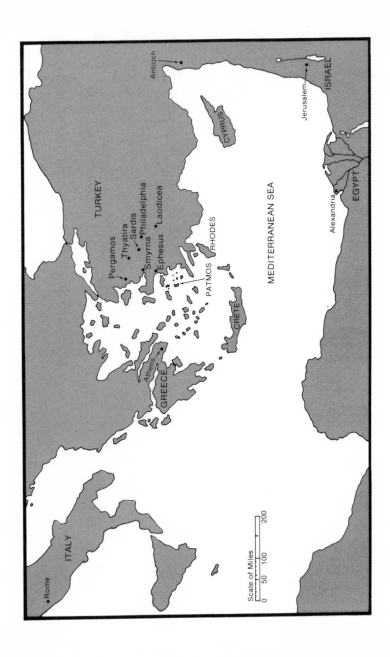

INTRODUCTION

The Book of Revelation is a book for our times. The closing book of the canon, it was written to describe events that will come to pass in the days just before the return of the Lord Jesus Christ. It opens with a vision of Christ and a series of letters written by John from Patmos to certain churches in the Roman province of Asia. The beloved apostle had been exiled to the island because of his faithfulness in preaching the Word of God and proclaiming the testimony of Christ (Rev. 1:9).

The place of writing. Patmos lies about thirty miles off the coast of modern Turkey, almost opposite the ancient city of Miletus. The island is about ten miles long and six miles wide at its widest point and has been under Greek control since World War II. Today its population is about twenty-five hundred. The Aegean island has a good harbor lined with small whitewashed houses. The highest point of the island is crowned by an eleventh-century Greek monastery built like a fortress and named after the apostle, St. John the Divine. Impressive from without with its lofty towers and crenellated walls, it is as picturesque and interesting within. The second floor contains a library of valuable ancient and medieval manuscripts, many of which have been carried off or sold through the centuries. The traveler today has a choice of riding a donkey or taking a taxi up the winding road from the harbor to the monastery where a spectacular view of the Aegean Sea awaits him from the monastery roof.

About halfway to the top of the island is a small monastery, gleaming white, built over a grotto said to be the cave where John received his revelation from God. Descending several flights of stairs, one finds himself in a cave heavily decorated in Greek Orthodox style with oil lamps suspended from the ceiling and quotations from the Apocalypse written on the walls. Although it cannot be proved that this was the exact place where John lived, the tradition is very old, and he undoubtedly lived in similar circumstances somewhere near this spot.

In John's day the island was probably not as attractive as it is today because of a sparse population, exposure to winds and storms, and complete isolation from the mainland where John longed to resume his ministry. Standing on top of the island on a clear day, John could see the top of the mountains of the mainland of Asia where his work and his heart were.

The place addressed. In 133 B.C. Attalus III, king of Pergamos, willed his kingdom to the Roman Empire. The Romans accepted the gift, and since it was their easternmost province at that time, they named it Asia or East. Its territory comprised one-third of the part of Turkey now known as Asia Minor. The gospel became known in this province of Asia through the preaching of Paul on his second and third missionary journeys, especially during the three years he spent at Ephesus (Acts 19:10). After Paul's death the Apostle John moved into the region and carried on the work. According to some early writers, he lived to be a very old man and finally died and was buried in Ephesus. Today the supposed site of his grave is marked in the ruins of a church that bears his name.

From the many churches in this area, the Lord picked out seven to receive a message through John. We know that there were more than just these seven churches in the province of Asia—Colosse and Hieropolis, for example. Therefore, the Lord must have had some special reason for addressing only these seven. The number seven is the number of completeness in the Bible, and the Book of Revelation is structured according to various sets of sevens. The seven churches addressed represent the whole province of Asia, but these specific churches were chosen instead of others because they had some special characteristics that Christ wanted to emphasize. Sir William Ramsay suggests that these seven churches were already known as distribution points for letters of Christian instruction and news, and that it would be understood that anything addressed to them would be intended for the whole province.[1] It must have been necessary to pass messages from the apostles and leaders in a systematic way so that the news would be certain to reach everyone. Forty years before, Paul had written a letter to the members of the church at Colosse, telling them, "When this epistle is read among you, cause that it be read also in the church of the Laodiceans; and that ye likewise read the epistle from Laodicea" (Col. 4:16). This exchange may have been the forerunner of the system that was developed. The churches are addressed in the order that a messenger would come to them from the island of Patmos. Landing at Miletus, the nearest port, he would make his way northward about twenty-five miles to Ephesus, thirty more to Smyrna, and sixty-five more to Pergamos. Then moving inland in a rough semicircle southeastward, he would reach Thyatira forty-five miles away and Sardis thirty miles

[1] William M. Ramsay, *The Letters to the Seven Churches of Asia* (London: Hodder & Stoughton, 1906), pp. 188-192.

Steven Lambright

farther south. Turning farther inland he would come to
Philadelphia about twenty-five miles away and eventually to Laodicea fifty miles beyond Philadelphia and
farthest from the coast.

The vision of Christ. As the book opens, the Apostle
John hears a voice. Turning to see who spoke, he sees
"one like unto the Son of Man" (Rev. 1:13). Although
many years have passed, John recognizes his beloved
Master whom he had known and followed. He sees the
Lord "clothed with a garment down to the foot, and
girt about the paps with a golden girdle" (1:13). This
long robe was an insignia of dignity and honor worn
by priests and judges. The girdle (belt) worn high,
instead of around the waist, favored a majestic, formal
movement. Like the rest of the description, the vision
is intended to present Christ as a majestic, all-powerful
Judge. John sees the Lord standing ready to judge His
church.

"His head and his hairs were white like wool, as
white as snow" (Rev. 1:14). This imagery is drawn from
Daniel 7:9, where Christ is called the "Ancient of
days." Although white hair is usually an indication of
feebleness and decay of old age, it certainly cannot
have this meaning here. White is the hottest kind of
heat, the extreme heat that purifies. White indicates
the purity of Christ as well as His duration of existence
and maturity of judgment.

"His eyes were as a flame of fire" (Rev. 1:14). The
appearance of the eyes like fire suggests knowledge of
all that is transpiring on earth. But more than knowing, these eyes look through and consume. Fire also is
an expression of anger (Heb. 10:27), which suggests
that Christ is ready to judge. Nothing is hid from Him,
but "all things are naked and opened unto the eyes of
him" (Heb. 4:13).

"His feet [were] like unto fine brass [i.e. bronze], as
if they burned in a furnace" (Rev. 1:15). Bronze is a

symbol of strength as well as of judgment in the Scriptures. The altar that portrayed judgment for sins was of bronze. The serpent lifted up in the wilderness to judge the Israelites' sin was of bronze. The metal imagery pictures the Lord as ready for judgment.

"His voice [was] as the sound of many waters" (Rev. 1:15). No sound gives such an impression of irresistible power as the crashing of waves upon the shore. John had ample opportunity to hear this sound on his island prison. The voice John heard was one of power and authority.

"Out of his mouth went a sharp two edged sword" (Rev. 1:16). This two-edged sword is a Thracian long sword used for cutting as well as thrusting, not the usual oriental sword. The sword is a symbol of authority and judgment as well as of the Word of God. Trench suggests that we have here an emblem of the "punishing power of the Word."[2]

General characteristics of the letters. The letters follow the same format and order of presentation:

1. A description of Christ. Each letter picks out and repeats certain appropriate portions of the description of Christ contained in the vision John saw of his Lord in chapter one.

2. A statement of the church's condition. Of the seven churches only two are condemned completely. Sardis is dead and Laodicea is rejected. Among the seven cities today only two are desolate and uninhabited, Sardis and Laodicea. Only two churches are praised without any condemnation, Smyrna and Philadelphia. In the many years of fierce fighting between Muslims and Christians that culminated in the Turkish conquest, the last two cities to fall to the Turks, long after the others had surrendered, were Smyrna and Philadelphia. One church, Ephesus, was

[2]Richard C. Trench, *Commentary on the Epistles to the Seven Churches in Asia* (London: Macmillan, 1883), p. 45.

told that it would be moved from its place, and Ephesus is the only city of the seven that has moved its location several miles inland. The remaining two churches received mixed praise and blame. These two cities, Pergamos and Thyatira, exist today as flourishing towns.

3. A call to repent. This call is for the five churches with defects.

4. A promise to overcomers. In each church, regardless of how deficient the Lord finds it, there were some individuals who had not given in to the temptation to sin. These the Lord calls *overcomers* and makes them certain promises of reward for continued faithfulness. All of the promises made in these letters look forward to and are explained by some reference in the later parts of the book. For example, the tree of life (Rev. 2:7) is mentioned again in 22:2. The second death (2:11) is mentioned in 20:14.

5. An exhortation to hear and heed the message. Twice it comes before the promise to the overcomers, but normally it comes last.

Each message is addressed to the "angel of the church." Many explanations of this term have been proposed. Some have said that the angel is the church. Others think that the angel is the personified spirit of the church. Still others think that since *angel* means *messenger* each church had a messenger or representative present to receive the letter from John and to bear it to its destination. Many take the angel to be a literal angel responsible to God as the guardian of the church. It is true that elsewhere in the Book of Revelation the word *angel* always refers to a literal heavenly creature; however, it seems pointless to write a letter to an angel blaming him for the defects in the church and then send the letter to the church and not to the angel. The majority of interpreters have felt that the reference is to the bishop or pastor, the person responsible for and in charge of the church. To him the letter is addressed, and he is blamed for error or indifference or praised for faithfulness and success in the church. An objection to this view similar to the one just mentioned might be raised: there is no evidence that the seven letters were ever sent separately to the individual churches or to the pastor of each church. All seven letters were incorporated into the rest of the book and sent to the province of Asia as a whole. It also seems unlikely that the church's letter was addressed to the pastor, since in the body of the letters it seems to be the church that is in view and really addressed, not just the pastor. The church is condemned for allowing false teaching or praised for standing fast. Individuals in the church are promised rewards. Since Revelation is a book of symbols (1:1), it may be that the Lord addressed an angel as representing the entire local church. "The church's individuality, its corporate unity, is expressed by the thought of a representative angel."[3] This view would remove the difficulty that elsewhere in the book angels are always literal heavenly creatures.

In his vision of Christ in chapter one, John turned and saw "seven golden candlesticks; and in the midst of the seven candlesticks one like unto the Son of Man" (Rev. 1:12-13). The King James Version uses the word "candlestick," but in John's day there were no candles as we know them today. A better translation is "lampstands." Notice that the Lord is in the midst of the churches. His presence unites them as one; empowers, encourages, and comforts; gives guidance and instruction; and shows His intimate knowledge of the exact condition of each church. The stars that represent the angels of the churches are in Christ's right hand (1:20). Their position shows the true relation between Christ and those who serve Him in the church. They have no authority of themselves or from the church but only such authority as they receive from Him. They have no

[3]F. J. A. Hort, *The Apocalypse of St. John* (London: Macmillan, 1908), p. 19.

power except as He gives it to them. In the hand of the Lord they have protection and safety.

The interpretation of the letters. Bible teachers have long pointed out that these seven letters may be interpreted in different ways. Just as the Book of Revelation as a whole has a meaning for us today in addition to its meaning for Christians of the first century, so these letters are not dry, abstract historical documents but living, vibrant messages from the Lord of the church to His church as a body and to its individual members. There is nothing outdated about them; they are as modern as drive-in churches. They are capable of bearing any and all of the following interpretations.

1. First, we must recognize that there were in Asia in John's day these seven cities containing these seven churches. Each church possessed the characteristics ascribed to it and was guilty of the Lord's accusations. The details of each letter had special significance for the church it addressed. The more we can find out about the historical conditions of the cities, the more we will know of the meaning of the letters for the churches to which they were addressed, and the better we will be able to interpret their meaning for the church of our day.

2. The letters also contain messages to other local churches from John's day to the present, for many churches since then have had the same virtues and faults that characterized Ephesus, Sardis, or Laodicea. For example, churches today that have tolerated false teachers need to heed the warnings given to these original churches.

3. Since seven is the number of completeness throughout the Book of Revelation, these seven churches represented the whole church of Asia and, in reality, the entire church of the New Testament world. Indeed, they portray the visible church of Christ on earth in any period of its history. The church of

today is a composite of the qualities, both good and bad, of these seven early churches.

4. Each of these seven letters closes with a message to individuals: "To him that overcometh"; "He that hath an ear, let him hear." There are valuable lessons in these chapters for Christians today. A church is made up of individuals and what its members are, the church is.

In addition, some have seen in the letters a history of the church written in advance. Starting with Ephesus, the Apostolic Age, they delineate the phases of church history to Laodicea, the church that typifies the apostate church existing at the end of the age when Christ returns. The usual correlation is as follows:

1. Ephesus—the Apostolic Age (to A.D. 100)
2. Smyrna—the period of persecution (100-300)
3. Pergamos—the early Middle Ages (300-1200)
4. Thyatira—the high Middle Ages (1200-1500)
5. Sardis—the Reformation period (1500-1700)
6. Philadelphia—the missionary period (1700-1900)
7. Laodicea—the present-day apostate church (1900 to the Second Coming).

A look at this listing reveals some interesting and obvious parallels. The first three periods match the first three churches quite well. For example, Smyrna was certainly a suffering church, and Laodicea, the last mentioned, is far from the Lord. In the others, however, the parallels are not so obvious, and some writers have proposed different systems of alignment. For example, Sardis is a church about which the Lord said nothing good. But is this church representative of the Reformation, which recovered and liberated the truths of the gospel from the bondage of Roman Catholicism? For this reason some have dated Pergamos 300-600, Thyatira 600-1200, and made Sardis the end of the Middle Ages, 1200-1500. Philadelphia then becomes the church of the Reformation period.

Several arguments have led some to reject this principle of assigning the churches to historical periods. First, the fact that interpreters have not been able to agree which church matches which period seems to prove that there is not enough real evidence to connect each church with a specific period of history. Second, advocates of this interpretation weaken their own case by having to admit that characteristics of one church (or period) carry over into later periods. For instance, traits of Sardis and Philadelphia characterize churches today. Third, most premillennialists who advocate this method of interpretation for chapters two and three are emphatic in denying the use of the same principle to interpret the remainder of the book. Fourth, premillennialists have traditionally taught that the return of Christ to raise the righteous dead and to rapture the living saints may take place at any time. This imminency is hard to reconcile with the idea that inspired Scripture sketches seven periods of church history that must elapse before Christ returns. In an appendix to his commentary on these epistles, R. C. Trench details the history of this interpretation and offers his objections to it. It seems best to think of every period of church history as containing elements that match all of the seven churches and not to tie any one of the letters to any one period of history.

EPHESUS: A LOVELESS CHURCH

"The first and greatest metropolis of Asia" is the title given to the city of Ephesus in some of its inscriptions. According to legend, when the founders of the city came to the mainland of Asia Minor, being uncertain where to settle, they consulted an oracle, which told them that a fish and a boar would show them the place. As they were cooking some fish, one fell out of the fire with a live coal attached and set fire to the brush. A boar hiding in the bushes fled in fright but was pursued and killed. Recalling the word of the oracle, the founders built the city on the spot where they killed the boar. For many years there stood beside the main street of Ephesus a statue of a boar commemorating this legend. This was the first city of Ephesus. Later the site of the city was moved several times, and the large, prosperous city of the first century was the third city to be built.

In Paul's day Ephesus was the chief Aegean port of Asia Minor, the gateway to the Orient from Greece and Rome. Also three major highways converged on Ephesus from the east—one from the Euphrates area through Laodicea, another from Galatia through Sardis, and a third from the south through the valley of the Meander River. Goods of every description funneled into Ephesus for shipment to points farther west, and sailors from many nations walked its streets and bought its wares. In Revelation 18 John lists the merchandise bought and sold in Babylon in the last days. John or Paul, shopping in the stores of Ephesus, would have found all of these articles offered for sale. Largely because of this trade the population of the city grew until it became the largest city in the entire region. Its population in the first century of the Christian era has been variously estimated by archaeologists as from two hundred thousand to three hundred thousand or more.

Rome had made Ephesus the practical capital of the province of Asia. As a free city, Ephesus granted its people such advantages as self-government and exemption from taxation. The city had its own magistrates called *Strategoi* and a governing body known as the *Boule*. Its main officer was called *Grammateus,* translated "town clerk" in the King James Version (Acts 19:35). He was not just a clerk but the chief administrator or city manager. Periodically the Roman governor came to town from Pergamos to try important cases since Ephesus was one of a series of towns where court was held in an arrangement similar to that of our circuit courts.

Each year Ephesus was host to the Pan-Ionian games, which rivaled the Olympics of Greece in prestige and importance. They were held in May and dedicated to Artemis (or Diana as the Romans called her). When Paul wrote to the Corinthians that he would stay in Ephesus until Pentecost (I Cor. 16:8), he might well have planned to capitalize on the presence of thousands of people from all over the province of Asia who came into the city to see the games. Paul wanted to witness to them (and perhaps also to see the games!). The public-spirited men who made the arrangements for the games and bore the cost were given the honorary title of *Asiarch.* Apparently one of these important men was converted to Christianity by Paul (Acts 19:31).

Next to its port, that which contributed most to the prosperity of Ephesus was its shrine dedicated to Artemis, one of the seven wonders of the ancient world. (The other six were the pyramids of Egypt, the Colossus of Rhodes, the statue of Zeus at Olympia, the hanging gardens of Babylon, the lighthouse at Alexandria, and the Mausoleum at Halicarnassus.) One ancient writer said that he had seen all of these wonders except the lighthouse, "but when I beheld the temple at Ephesus towering to the clouds all these other marvels were eclipsed."[4] Pilgrims came from all over the world to worship in the temple and to buy images of Artemis and charms reputed to have great powers to heal and to work other miracles. The story is told of an Olympic wrestler whom no one could throw because he was wearing a charm from the temple of Artemis around his ankle. When it was removed, he was no stronger or better than any other man. The Roman Catholic church, with its medals and tokens from the saints, has taken over the pagan customs of Ephesus. Instead of the name of Artemis, the name of some saint is carved on the object. The Jews do not have these images; the Muslims certainly do not tolerate images in their worship; Protestants never use them. Outside of pagan heathenism, only the Roman Catholic church practices idolatry.

An earlier temple had burned in 365 B.C. (according to the story) on the night that Alexander the Great was born. It was rebuilt over a number of years. When Alexander came to Ephesus as a young man, he offered to pay for the completion of the temple, but the citizens declined the offer, not wanting his control, and finished it by their own resources. This magnificent structure, twice the size of the Parthenon, stood until

[4]W.A. Criswell, *Expository Sermons on Revelation*, V. 2 (Grand Rapids: Zondervan, 1963), p. 68.

A.D. 263, when the city was sacked by the Goths. The temple proper was 425 feet in length (longer than a football field) and 225 feet wide. Its roof was supported by 127 columns 60 feet high. In the temple was a huge statue of Artemis thought by some to have been carved from a meteorite because of the reference in Acts 19:35 to a stone fallen from heaven. The early settlers of Ephesus had taken over the worship of an Anatolian goddess, Cybele, and combined it with the Greek worship of Artemis. Artemis, originally a goddess of the hunt, merged with Cybele, a mother goddess whose worship was a fertility cult. Instead of the lovely graceful statues of the Greeks and Romans, Artemis of Ephesus is squat and ugly. Statues of her have been uncovered in the ruins both with and without a tall headdress. Her upper body is covered with oval-shaped objects, variously interpreted as breasts, dates, or eggs, all symbols of fertility. Hundreds of priests and priestesses served in the temple, and prostitution was part of the worship.

The temple had a rear room used as a treasury that served also as a bank where individuals, businesses, and even governments kept their money and valuables. Tremendous wealth was accumulated in the treasury for safekeeping since no one would think of desecrating a sacred building by stealing anything within its precincts. On one occasion, Ephesus was captured and plundered by a rival state; but being also a worshiper of Artemis, it left the temple untouched. Rome had given the temple the right of sanctuary; and, therefore, no one within bowshot distance (about two hundred yards) of the temple could be arrested for any crime or avenged by anyone seeking his life. Consequently, many criminals lived close to the temple. Strange combination—a bank surrounded by criminals! These wicked, lawless men, mingling with the prostitute priestesses, made the environment of the temple very degenerate.

Today nothing is left of the temple. Archaeologists searched for years before locating the site. It was discovered in a low swampy area some distance from the ruins of the city, covered with fifteen to twenty feet of accumulated dirt and rubbish. A few of the columns may be seen today in Istanbul, where they were carried for use in the building of the Saint Sophia church; some are in the British Museum. Restoration is still going on.

Extensive excavations in the city have uncovered a number of important and interesting buildings dating from the first centuries of the Christian era. In spite of the great amount of work that has been done, it is estimated that the present diggings comprise only one-twentieth of the city. One of the most interesting buildings connected with the New Testament is the great theater. The original theater was constructed about 300 B.C. in the Greek style, but its present Romanized form shows that it was renovated in the first century of this era; construction was probably in progress when the angry mob of silversmiths rioted and stormed into the theater shouting, "Great is Diana of the Ephesians" (Acts 19:34). The main changes were in the stage and rooms beneath and behind it to provide for changes in the manner of presenting the plays. The acoustics were excellent, and the theater seated more than twenty thousand people. The top of the theater provides an excellent view of the city. The main street, known as the Arcadian street, runs from the front of the theater to the ancient harbor, which can be seen from the higher seats.

In Paul's day Ephesus had begun a process of decline that would continue until the city was completely abandoned. The Cayster River, which flowed by the city, was bringing silt into the area and filling the harbor. Many ships, especially the larger ones, were going a few miles north to the fine harbor of Smyrna (modern Izmir). A century before Paul, engineers were conducting dredging operations to keep the harbor open. However, it was a losing battle, for the river gradually brought about the death of the city. As the harbor filled up, the area became swampy and unhealthy and eventually forced the city to be abandoned. The inhabitants moved to higher ground away from the water. Without a harbor Ephesus slowly died.

Today the Aegean Sea is miles from the ruins of the city. The remains of a church marking the supposed grave of the Apostle John stands on the site of the fourth city of Ephesus. From this high hill one can see in the valley below the location of the famed temple of Artemis.

One of the last noteworthy events in the city's history was the meeting of the great ecumenical synod in A.D. 431 in a church dedicated to the Virgin Mary. It was in this meeting that the church officially declared for the first time that Mary was the "Mother of God." Ruins of this church may be seen not far from those of the great theater.

Ephesus today is a deserted ruin. Tourists roam its excavated streets, but no one lives there. For centuries it has lain undisturbed and useless. Nearby is a small village, the fifth city of Ephesus, called Seljuk by the Turks. The light is gone; the candlestick is removed; the words of warning of Revelation 2:5 have been fulfilled.

Each of the letters to the seven churches begins with a detail of John's vision of Christ in chapter one that is appropriate to the church addressed. To Ephesus, Christ is pictured as holding the seven stars in His hand and walking in the midst of the seven golden lampstands. This indicates a close relationship of fellowship and protection with this church. Barclay points out that the use of the accusative case after the word "hold," instead of the usual genitive case, emphasizes that Christ holds the entire church, not just a part of it. No one group or denomination has exclusive rights to the Lord.[5]

The letter proper begins with the statement "I know thy works" (Rev. 2:2). The writer of Hebrews says, "Neither is there any creature that is not manifest in his sight: but all things are naked and opened unto the eyes of him with whom we have to do" (4:13). There is nothing quicker in an angel's wing or a lightning flash than the speed with which all things are telegraphed to the ear and understanding of the divine Saviour. It is a comforting thought that no Christian does anything for his Lord that He does not know. Good works will not pass unnoticed and unrewarded. "For whosoever shall give you a cup of water to drink in my name, because ye belong to Christ, verily I say unto you, he shall not lose his reward" (Mark 9:41). No suffering or hardship is endured of which He is not sympathetically aware. It is also a sobering thought that any neglect or indifference is open to His gaze. No sin or backsliding, however small or secret, can be hidden from Him.

The Works of the Church

This perfect knowledge reveals many good things about the Ephesian church. First, it was *a working church:* "I know thy works, and thy labour" (2:2), or, as some would translate it, "I know thy works, even thy labour." The word translated "labour" (*kopos*) is not redundant with the word translated "works"; it stresses the effort that goes into work, "thy toil" (cf. 14:13: "That they may rest from their labours"; I Cor. 15:58: "your labour is not in vain"). Labor is what produces work. Nothing is accomplished for Christ without effort—tiresome, exhausting effort. These Ephesian Christians were willing to expend time and energy for Christ and for His cause, willing to

[5]William Barclay, *The Letters to the Seven Churches* (London: SCM, 1957), p. 21.

attempt difficult tasks. Someone has said, "Christianity has not been tried and found wanting. It has been
found hard and not tried." In performing their work,
the Ephesians had patience. They did not become discouraged and quit but persevered. "[Thou] hast not
fainted" (i.e. "grown weary"; cf. "let us not be weary in
well doing," Gal. 6:9). This church had been known as
a growing church (Acts 19:10, 20). Its members were
not content to see the same faces every week. They
were not satisfied to feed the same few Christians until
they were fat with inactivity without making an effort
to reach the lost. Just as the tallest trees grow in the
thickest forest, so spiritual growth is greatest where
evangelism is adding new Christians to the church.

In the second place the church at Ephesus was *a
well-taught church.* "I know ... how thou canst not
bear them which are evil: and thou hast tried them
which say they are apostles, and are not, and hast
found them liars" (2:2); "This thou hast, that thou
hatest the deeds of the Nicolaitanes, which I also hate"
(2:6). These Christians could distinguish truth from
error. In a letter to Ephesus about A.D. 110, fifteen
or twenty years after John had written, Ignatius tes-
tified to the church's orthodoxy: "Indeed Onesimus
himself gives great praise to your good order in God for
you all live according to the truth; and no heresy dwells
among you: nay, you do not even listen to any unless
he speak concerning Jesus Christ in truth. I have
learned, however, that some from elsewhere have
stayed with you, who have evil doctrine: but you did
not suffer them to sow it among you, and stopped your
ears, so that you might not receive what they sow" (*To
the Ephesians* 6. 2; 60. 1).[6] Churches today would do
well to be as vigilant and intolerant of error, instead of
broad-mindedly listening to the tempting suggestions
of the devil and ending up deceived by him.

[6]Ignatius, *Epistle to the Ephesians*, 6. 2; 60. 1.

The exact nature of the group called Nicolaitans has been a mystery. They may have derived their name from someone named Nicholas who started their special teaching. Some have suggested that the name means "conqueror of the people" from *nikao* and *laos* and that the cult advocated a ruling priesthood. But the fact that one word looks like another does not mean that it comes from it. Instead, the name probably indicates the similarity of its teaching to the doctrine of Balaam in the Old Testament, for the name may be a Greek equivalent of *Balaam*. In Revelation 2:14-15 Balaam and the Nicolaitans are mentioned together. As Balaam taught the Israelites to compromise with the pagan civilizations around them, so the Nicolaitans may have worked out some compromise between Christianity and the Roman imperial worship. A person could hardly live in the world of the first century without coming into constant contact with paganism. If he ate with his neighbor or attended a banquet or party, the food was probably dedicated to the gods. Service in the army required attendance at pagan rituals. The eagles, standards of the Roman army, were of the nature of idols. If a person held office, he had to participate in the formalities of idol and emperor worship. Evidently the Nicolaitans had worked out some sort of accommodation in their doctrinal teaching to enable them to be Christians and citizens of the world at the same time. They avoided participation in the more extreme practices of paganism but saw no harm in the formalities in order to hold office, belong to clubs, and get along in the world. They taught, plausibly, that these acts were merely expressions of patriotism that did not interfere with their Christian faith. Theirs was a broad view, a tolerant view, that would, they reasoned, allow Christianity to continue to exist, to prosper, to expand, and to influence its neighbors for good. This view Christ unequivocally rejects: "which [deeds] I also hate"

(2:6). Sir William Ramsay says: "Nothing could have saved the infant church from melting away into one of those vague and ineffective schools of philosophic ethics except the stern and strict rule that is laid down here by St. John. An easy-going Christianity could never have survived; it could not have conquered and trained the world; only the most convinced, resolute, almost bigoted adherence to the most uncompromising interpretation of its own principles could have given the Christians the courage and self-reliance that were needed. For them to hesitate or to doubt was to be lost."[7]

The church at Ephesus had discrimination. It tested and disapproved those who were making false claims. In his First Epistle (probably written from Ephesus to the surrounding region) John warns, "Believe not every spirit, but try the spirits whether they are of God" (4:1). There are two tests for discerning false teachers: their doctrine (Gal. 1:8; I John 4:2) and their lives (Matt. 7:16). The church applied these tests and refused to have anything to do with evil men. They did not honor apostates. The Ephesians could bear persecution, but they could not bear evil men (2:3). They had experienced the fulfillment of Jesus' warning in the Olivet discourse: "Ye shall be hated of all nations for my name's sake" (Matt. 24:9). We need churches today that will not compromise with evil and Christians who cannot be deceived by false teachings, who have the courage to separate from and have nothing to do with those who are preaching and practicing compromise, and who will endure being avoided and even hated by the society around them. Ephesus was a strict church, not a soft one.

The Waning of Love

What more would one expect to find in a church? A pastor today would consider himself fortunate to have

[7]Ramsay, p. 300.

a church like that of the Ephesians. But the omniscient Lord saw one thing defective, one point at which the church was lacking, one bad quality that threatened to negate all of the good ones: "I have somewhat against thee because thou hast left thy first love" (2:4). The word "somewhat" in the King James Version is in italics because it is not in the original Greek. A more exact translation is, "I have against thee because thou hast lost thy first love." Losing one's first love is not a trivial matter but something very serious. These people had come to Christ out of paganism. They were Christians not because of custom or fashion but because of a love for Christ and His power to save. But, alas, truths once so bright and thrilling to the soul may become soiled by handling, losing their freshness and power. The Ephesians had themselves fulfilled another prophecy of the Lord's Olivet discourse: "Because iniquity shall abound, the love of many shall wax cold" (Matt. 24:12). The word rendered "many" may be translated "the many" or "the majority." In Ephesus the majority had grown cold. The trouble was not zeal; the Ephesians were hard workers. The trouble was not doctrine; they were sound in the faith. The trouble was devotion. The machinery was still moving under the power of the original impulse, but the great moving spirit was losing its force. As Vance Havner says, "One may be as straight as a gun barrel theologically and as empty as a gun barrel spiritually."[8] A young lover will buy his beloved a gift he cannot afford, thinking not of the cost but of pleasing the one he loves. It was not Mary of Bethany but Judas who thought of the cost of the perfume she poured on Christ. Love was the difference.

Newlyweds are interesting to watch. They long to be together constantly; they talk about the bliss of wedded life; they like to praise the virtues of their mate. Is this our relationship to Christ? Do we long for and enjoy

[8]Vance Havner, *Repent or Else!* (New York: Revell, 1958), p. 25.

fellowship with Him? Do we speak of the joy and peace of the Christian life and praise the excellencies of our beloved Lord? Love should grow richer and deeper as the months and years go by. It is true that as we grow older the youthful effervescence tends to wane, but it should give way to a more firmly settled purpose and conviction to move forward. The leaping, sparkling rill may lose its dash and hurry but only to widen and deepen into the river, still moving steadily on toward the great ocean. Alas, oftentimes the original love is not increased or even sustained. A husband or wife may continue to perform faithfully the duties of providing a living or caring for a home when all of the affectionate devotion has left the marriage.

> A boy and girl walk down the street.
> She trips. He murmurs, "Careful sweet."
> They wed and tread the selfsame street.
> She trips. He growls, "Pick up your feet."

The first love has been the theme of songwriters down through the ages. "More love to Thee, O Christ, more love to Thee. Hear thou the prayer I make on bended knee" (Elizabeth Prentis). "Spirit of God, descend upon my heart, Wean it from earth, through all its pulses move. Stoop to my weakness, mighty as Thou art, And make me love Thee as I ought to love. Teach me to love Thee as Thine angels love, One holy passion filling all my frame; the baptism of the heaven-descended Dove, My heart an altar, and Thy love the flame" (George Croly).

The Way of Restoration

What can be done about lost love? The Lord commands three acts as steps to restoration. The first is *remember*. "Remember therefore from whence thou art fallen" (Rev. 2:5). We should remind ourselves of what Christ has done for us, of all the past blessings that have been our portion. The prophet Jeremiah voices God's complaint against Israel: "I remember thee, the kindness of thy youth, the love of thine espousals, when thou wentest after me in the wilderness, in a land that was not sown. ... What iniquity have your fathers found in me, that they are gone far from me and have walked after vanity, and are become vain?" (Jer. 2:2-5). The prodigal came to himself and said, "How many hired servants of my father's have bread enough and to spare, and I perish with hunger!" (Luke 15:17). The first step back to God is to realize how far we have fallen.

The second step is to *repent*. One sin, if unchecked, will lead to others. Divorce never comes until love has been lost. But true repentance is not merely from a recognition of the consequences of sin but from guilt: a sense of the wrong of it. Pharaoh said, "Take away the frogs from me" (Exod. 8:8), but he did not repent and let the Israelites go. David said, "My sin is ever before me" (Ps. 51:3). If we truly repent, we will not plunge back into sin the next day. We must confess our cold indifference, our lack of love for God, and determine by God's grace to put it away forever. There must be a change of direction in the life.

The third command is to *repeat*. "Do the first works" (2:5). We do many things from necessity or a sense of duty whether we feel like it or not. But it is better to work from devotion. Whereas the trained nurse will stay with her patient all night because she is paid to do so, the mother watches over her sick child all night because she loves him. This doing of the first works is the only proof of the genuineness of our repentance.

Even when love has grown cold there is still some hope. The Spirit issues a challenge: "To him that overcometh will I give to eat of the tree of life, which is in the midst of the paradise of God" (2:7). The paradise of God is contrasted with the splendor of the temple of Artemis, that wonder of the ancient world. A dying church is pointed to the tree of life. Having disappeared after man sinned and was driven from Eden, it reappears in the New Jerusalem after sin is eliminated and the last enemy, death, is destroyed. The one who overcomes will be with Christ in the New Jerusalem for eternity.

The word "overcomer" implies a conflict. No one gets to heaven without fighting his way through enemy country. This world lies in the wicked one. Satan is its prince. We are strangers and sojourners, and the devil will not let us pass without a fight.

> Must I be carried to the skies on flowery beds of
> ease,
> While others fought to win the prize, and sailed
> through bloody seas?
> Are there no foes for me to face? Must I not stem
> the flood?
> Is this vile world a friend to grace, to help me on
> to God?
> Sure I must fight if I would reign; increase my cour-
> age, Lord;
> I'll bear the toil, endure the pain supported by Thy
> Word.

Ephesus. Portion of the ancient forum (marketplace) (top). Ephesus. Doorway to Roman building (bottom left). Smyrna. Forum showing lower level shops (bottom right).

Pergamos. Hospital dedicated to the worship of Asklepios with the acropolis (high city) in the background.

Thyatira. Roman building (top). Sardis. Portion of the royal road. Main highway from Persia to the coast. In use several hundred years before Christ (bottom).

Philadelphia. Remains of ancient city wall (top). Laodicea. Roman theater as it appears today (bottom).

SMYRNA: A SUFFERING CHURCH

The third largest city in Turkey today is Izmir. A city of 250,000 to 275,000, it is a very busy port and manufacturing center. The modern city is the site of ancient Smyrna. Its rival ports, Ephesus and Miletus, lost their harbors through the silting action of their rivers and long ago fell into decay and disuse. Smyrna continues a thriving and important city.

The origin of Smyrna is lost in antiquity. It seems to have existed since the beginning of civilization in Asia Minor. The city sits at the end of a sheltered gulf reaching thirty-five miles inland, into which the Hermos River empties its flow and from which a famous highway leads up the river valley past Sardis into the interior of Anatolia—a natural location for a city. Its name derives from its trade in the herb myrrh, which was widely used as an anesthetic and embalming substance. The word *smurna* occurs in the New Testament in Matthew 2:11, John 19:39, and (in a verb form) Mark 15:23.

The old Greek settlement was destroyed by the Lydians around 600 B.C. and lay in ruins with only a few scattered inhabitants in the vicinity until the time of Alexander the Great. According to Pausanias, Alexander had been hunting on Mount Pagos and was resting under a tree when a goddess appeared to him and instructed him to build a city there. The work was begun by Alexander and carried on after his death by his successors until Smyrna became a model Greek city. Mount Pagos with its temples and buildings was referred to as the "crown of Smyrna." Its streets were broad and well paved. The golden street, as it was called, began at the harbor and ran up the mountain to the acropolis at the top of Pagos. It was lined with temples of Cybelle, Apollo, Asklepios, and Aphrodite, and on the summit rose one dedicated to Zeus. Strabo, the geographer, called Smyrna the most beautiful of all cities.

Smyrna was also a political center. Its rulers seem to have had the gift of political foresight, for as wars were waged and armies moved back and forth across Asia Minor, Smyrna unfailingly chose to support the winning side. Long before anyone else in the East paid much attention to Rome, Smyrna formed a friendly alliance with her. About 195 B.C. Smyrna built the first temple in Asia to the cult of deified Rome. These and other acts of ingratiation were called to the emperor's attention in A.D. 26, and Smyrna was chosen from a number of competing cities for the privilege of erecting a temple in honor of Tiberius. Rome did not forget her faithful ally in other ways, and Smyrna was made a free city, possessing its own government and remaining partially exempt from imperial taxation. It was a center of the Roman judicial system, where Roman judges sat to try cases from the surrounding district.

Emperor worship (or worship of Rome as epitomized in the emperor) arose to meet a need. Rome's far-flung, heterogeneous empire, consisting of many peoples of greatly diverse cultures, languages, and customs, needed something to unify the subject nations. This something was religion. Rome had brought many advantages to the nations it had conquered—an extensive system of good roads, the so-called "Roman peace" with the cessation of inter-tribal wars and the elimination of pirates and bandits, the Roman system of justice, and a measure of prosperity—all of which might elicit from the people not only gratitude but also worship of the power that had provided all these blessings.

The first emperors did not take their deification very seriously, regarding it merely as a matter of political expediency. However, under later reigns emperor worship became not only a sign of patriotism but a test of loyalty, and refusal to worship at the emperor's shrine was considered an act of treason. Once a year every citizen was expected to burn incense on the altar at the emperor's temple. There is extant a request for a certificate showing that a recipient had performed his sacrifice and was free of obligation for the year.

> To those who have been appointed to preside over the sacrifices, from Inares Akeus, from the village of Theoxenis, together with his children, Aias and Hera, who reside in the village of Theadelphia. We have always sacrificed to the gods, and now, in your presence, according to the regulations, we have sacrificed and offered libations, and tasted the sacred things, and we ask you to give us a certification that we have done so. May you fare well.

The certificate reads, "We, the representatives of the Emperor, Serenos, and Hermas, have seen you sacrificing."[9]

Once a citizen had made his yearly sacrifice, he could worship any other god or gods he chose. All the Christian had to do was appear in the temple, burn his incense, and repeat the formula "Caesar is lord." But this is exactly what the Christians refused to do. The name *lord* (*kurios*) was a term reserved for Christ. "Christ is Lord" meant to them "Christ is God." It

[9]Barclay, p. 33.

would have been gross idolatry to give this name to Caesar. Therefore, they chose to be considered disloyal to Rome and to become subject to persecution.

One famous leader to die because of this custom was Polycarp, the bishop of Smyrna. In A.D. 155, he was brought before the authorities and given the choice of worshiping Caesar or being put to death. The proconsul pleaded with him to save his life by denying Christ and promised to set him free. Polycarp replied, "Eighty and six years have I served him, and he never did me wrong. How then can I blaspheme my King and Saviour?" Although it happened on the Sabbath, the Jews were so eager to see him die they violated their own Sabbath laws by carrying wood into the stadium for the fire. That afternoon Polycarp was burned to death. This persecution was coming on the church when John wrote his letter about sixty years earlier. Polycarp, still a young man, may have been one of the members addressed in the letter.

The origin of the church at Smyrna is not known. Probably while Paul was at Ephesus and the gospel was spreading "so that all they which dwelt in Asia heard the word of the Lord" (Acts 19:10), some converts started this church. Its testimony continued into the Middle Ages. Smyrna was one of the last cities in Asia Minor to fall to the Turks and the Muslim faith.

Smyrna was the most severely persecuted of the seven churches to which John wrote. To these beleaguered Christians the Lord pictures Himself as the one "which was dead, and is alive" (2:8). The city of Smyrna had experienced a resurrection: after it had lain in ruins for several centuries, Alexander the Great had rebuilt it, and the city lived again. Now as these Christians faced death, they were encouraged by the fact that He for whom they were about to die had Himself passed through death and triumphed over it by a resurrection. Just as the mother who has lost a child can understand, sympathize with, and console another woman who is passing through the same experience, so Christ can understand and help His people facing death because He has faced it and conquered it.

Comfort

"I know thy ... tribulation, and poverty" (2:9). What caused this tribulation? The numerous Jews in the city very probably caused the Christians trouble. Everywhere the gospel went, the Jews banded together to oppose it with all their energy and influence. They had great influence with the authorities. Their hatred of Christianity in Smyrna is shown by their conduct in the martyrdom of Polycarp. As Paul says, blindness is come upon them because of their rejection of Christ (Romans 11:7, 8, 25). The Lord says, "I know the blasphemy of them which say they are Jews, and are not, but are the synagogue of Satan" (Rev. 2:9). These were Jews by race (physical descendants of Abraham, Isaac, and Jacob) but they were not true Jews (spiritual Israel) because they had rejected their Messiah. As Paul says again, "For they are not all Israel, which are of Israel. ... They which are the children of the flesh, these are not the children of God" (Rom. 9:6-8). These Jews in their opposition to Christ and his church were guilty of blasphemy in denying the person of Christ. Their assembly was not a place for the worship of God but a synagogue belonging to and controlled by Satan (2:9).

Another probable cause was the cult of emperor worship, lack of participation in which could bring the Christians to trial before the magistrates for disloyalty to the Roman government. The word *tribulation* means "pressure." These Christians were caught between the Jews and the pagans as if between the jaws of a nutcracker or between the upper and lower stones of a giant millstone. The opposition of these groups brought poverty to the Christians at Smyrna. Their stores were boycotted; they were not permitted to sell; they could not get jobs. Sometimes they were robbed and their possessions confiscated (Heb. 10:34). The word used for poverty, *ptocheia,* means "extreme poverty," the condition of having nothing at all. The apostle could have used another Greek word, *penes,* which means simply "poor," having nothing extra (cf. their uses in II Cor. 8:2, 9, and 9:9).

We have seen a parallel in our own times. Before the Second World War in Japan the government was insisting that all the people, and especially all school children, participate in ceremonies giving worship to the emperor as the head of the state. Some Christian leaders pointed out that this was merely an expression of patriotism somewhat like saluting the flag in our country. Others insisted that it was an act of idolatry and therefore should be resisted by Christians at all costs. Those who took this hard inflexible position saw their converts survive and prosper while those who allowed emperor worship by their converts saw them drift back into their old paganism.

"I know," He says, "your tribulation and poverty." Christ knows the suffering of His saints, not only by virtue of His omniscience but also as that which He has either sent or permitted. No tribulation or hardship can come into the life of a Christian that Christ does not allow. Peter, writing to this same region a few years earlier, said, "Let them that suffer *according to the will of God* commit the keeping of their souls to him in well doing" (I Peter 4:19; emphasis added). Christ knows our need of hardship to help us develop. A wise parent does not work his child's homework for him; the child must learn to do it himself. He does not give the child everything he wants and asks for; the child must learn to earn his own way, to distinguish what is necessary and good from what is not, to do without when necessary. Sometimes parents let the child try something they know he cannot do to teach

him to ask advice. Suffering drives us to God. When
my boys were young, they would play outside for hours
with no thought of mother or home. When called in for
a meal, they would be reluctant to come because they
were enjoying their play. But as soon as one of them
got hurt, he would head for home and mother. So it
is with us. God knows that too much prosperity and
pleasure is bad for us. Feeling self-sufficient, we
easily forget Him. Persecution reminds us of our
weakness and need and turns us to Him for help and
comfort.

Christ's knowledge of our suffering enables Him to
sympathize with us. He knows not only with His mind
but also with His heart. He feels for and with us. When
the Lord appeared to Saul on the road to Damascus,
His words were, "Saul, Saul, why persecutest thou
me?" (Acts 9:5; emphasis added). When the Christian suffers, Christ suffers. There are interesting parallels between the sufferings of Christ and those of
the Christians of Smyrna. Christ suffered for a cause.
His persecution was instigated and directed by Jewish
leaders in collaboration with pagan gentile leaders
whom they had stirred up to oppose the Lord. He died
the lingering death of a criminal. So Christ knows their
difficulty because He had been through the same experi-
ences. His knowledge extends beyond the present to
the future. In Smyrna there was uncertainty; the Christians were not sure what suffering they might have to
endure. Christ knew perfectly what lay ahead of Him
and when it would come. He prayed in the garden that
the cup might pass from Him but knew as He prayed
that God's will must be done. Before His death He told
the disciples, "In the world ye shall have tribulation:
but be of good cheer; I have overcome the world" (John
16:33). He endured suffering and death and triumphed
over them and now stands ready to help His saints
who face the same trials. It is no wonder the writer
of Hebrews rejoiced in the assurance that "we might

have a strong consolation, who have fled for refuge to lay hold upon the hope set before us: which hope we have as an anchor of the soul, both sure and steadfast, and which entereth into that within the veil; whither the forerunner is for us entered, even Jesus" (Heb. 6:18-20).

Commendation

There are no words of direct commendation for this church, only the indirect praise in the statement "thou art rich" (2:9). Nothing is said to be wrong with this church. It is interesting that of the seven churches the only two that are not criticized for some defect are the two with the most difficulty and the least outward size and prestige. Somehow suffering seems to have a purifying effect. Perhaps this church did not need lavish praise. Some people are so constituted that they need praise and encouragement to give them assurance and confidence. Others are strong enough that they do not need it. G. Campbell Morgan tells the story of a woman who dreamed she saw three women kneeling in prayer. The Lord appeared, and stopping beside the first, He spoke tender words of encouragement to her. As He passed the second, He placed His hand on her head and smiled at her. But the third He passed with hardly a glance in her direction. The woman who dreamed thought to herself, "The Lord must certainly love this first woman, and she must be very close to him to receive such favorable treatment. And the second woman must have nothing wrong with her, for the Lord is certainly not angry with her. But the last woman! She must have done something to greatly displease Him to be treated so." At this point the Lord turned to the dreamer and said, "You have judged wrongly. The first woman needs all of my care to keep her from going astray. The second woman has stronger faith. The third woman whom I passed with little notice has the highest love and the greatest faith of the three and will remain true to me independently of words or looks."[10] Special attentions indicate weakness and need on the part of the recipient rather than strength.

These Christians were destitute but rich. God has "chosen the poor of this world [to be] rich in faith" (James 2:5). Paul describes himself as "poor, yet making many rich" (II Cor. 6:10). To the church at Laodicea the Lord says, "Thou sayest, I am rich, and increased with goods, and have need of nothing; and knowest not that thou art wretched, and miserable, and poor, and blind, and naked" (Rev. 3:17). There is a difference between saying "I am rich" and being rich. Laodicea was rich materially but poverty-stricken spiritually. No man is any richer than his soul. John wrote to Gaius wishing him to prosper materially even as his soul prospered (III John 2). Christ told the story of the rich man who died full of material wealth but without having made provision for his spiritual needs. The Lord called him a fool (Luke 12:20). Of course Smyrna was not rich spiritually merely because it was poor materially; some men have treasure neither in heaven nor on earth. These early Christians were rich in that they possessed a Saviour who had forgiven their sins and had convictions worth dying for. They possessed a quality of life that death could not destroy.

Counsel

Christ not only knew their past persecutions and their poverty, but He knew that there was still more to come. Things would get worse before they got better. So as He encourages them, he counsels them to faithfulness. "Fear none of those things which thou shalt suffer: behold, the devil shall cast some of you into

---

[10]G. Campbell Morgan, *The Letters of Our Lord* (London: Pickering & Ingles, nd), p. 35.

prison, that ye may be tried; and ye shall have tribulation ten days" (2:10). God never promises His people an easy time. When Christ was on earth, He did not offer His followers a flower-strewn path of prosperity and outward peace. Theologians refer to the church on earth as the "church militant." The Christian life is a battle, an athletic contest, a struggle. These analogies are applicable not just to first-century Christianity but also to the Christian life today; we can expect the same treatment if we are the kind of Christians we ought to be. In Smyrna the trouble had come from the devil just as had Job's suffering many centuries earlier. The men who opposed the believers were Satanic agents. The period, ten days, has been variously interpreted. Some suggest that the number ten indicates a time of testing, as it seems to in Daniel 1:11-15 and Jeremiah 42:7. More often it is explained as a short time, mercifully limited by God and soon to be past. If there was any literal significance to the number ten in connection with the persecution of the church, we do not know what it was.

The Lord's counsel was twofold: "fear not" and "be thou faithful unto death" (2:10). At the time John wrote, prison sentences were not in use as a punishment for crime; prisons were for those awaiting trial or execution. It is clear that the imprisonment mentioned was a prelude to execution and that the Lord is implying that some of these Christians will suffer martyrdom. Be not afraid of death, the Scripture urges. Christ has died and risen from the dead. He has passed through the dark valley before us. We need no longer fear death as the great unknown. We have a guide to conduct us to the other side. To be absent from the body is to be present with the Lord. "Forasmuch then as the children are partakers of flesh and blood, he also himself likewise took part of the same; that through death he might destroy him that had the power of death, that is, the devil; and deliver them who through fear of death were all their lifetime subject to bondage" (Heb. 2:14, 15).

"Be thou faithful unto death" seems to mean in this context, "Be willing to die. Do not deny the Lord." Down through the years the city of Smyrna had been faithful to her master, Rome. Now the Christians of Smyrna are told to be faithful to their master, Christ. The word *faith* may also have the idea of trust. "In this time of testing put your trust in Me. Depend on Me. I will see you through." To people living in the United States in the twentieth century, these circumstances may seem distant and unreal. But in parts of the world today Christians are being persecuted, even losing their lives for their faith. Will Christians in the United States ever be subjected to the trials being undergone by their brethren in China and Russia today? We pray not. But if tribulation does come, if God does see fit to permit us to suffer, these words to Smyrna will bring strength and comfort.

Conquest

"I will give thee a crown of Life" (2:16). In the New Testament, two words are translated "crown": *diadema* is the crown of royalty worn by kings and emperors and by the Lord (19:12); *stephanos* is a wreath made of laurel or another kind of leaves. The latter was awarded to winners in athletic contests; it was worn at weddings and other celebrations; and, in Smyrna, it was given to officials as a reward for faithful service to the government. Coins from Smyrna show rulers wearing this crown of leaves. The peak of Mount Pagos, the acropolis of the city, was referred to by some of the ancient writers as the *stephanos* of Smyrna. To the Christian who wins the victory, to the one who is faithful, the Lord promises not merely a crown of beauty and honor but a crown (*stephanos*) of life. James writes, "Blessed is the man that endureth temptation: for when he is tried, he shall receive the crown of life, which the Lord hath promised to them that love him" (James 1:12).

To the Christian who remains faithful, there is another promise: "He that overcometh shall not be hurt of the second death" (2:11). These Christians were facing physical death. The rewards promised them emphasize victory over death, a crown of life, and immunity from the second death. Physical death was the worst punishment that unbelievers could inflict on the saints. There is something far worse: "And death and hell were cast into the lake of fire. This is the second death" (Rev. 20:14). All who leave this life without faith in Jesus Christ must face a second death worse than the first. As punishment for their sins and for the rejection of the Son of God, they will be placed for eternity in the lake of fire. Jesus said, "Fear not them which kill the body, but are not able to kill the soul: but rather fear him which is able to destroy both soul and body in hell" (Matt. 10:28). If men and women today would fear the second death as much as they seek to postpone the first, there would be a great turning to God in our land. These words of warning to the persecutors are words of comfort to the persecuted. The persecuted Christians may die, but they will not be defeated. They need not fear the pain of the first death because they will never be hurt by the fire of the second. What words could have done more to strengthen and encourage them? Faithfulness to Christ may bring death on earth but it brings life for eternity. The principle is enunciated by Paul— "While we look not at the things which are seen, but at the things which are not seen: for the things which are seen are temporal; but the things which are not seen are eternal" (II Cor. 4:18)—and by the Lord Himself while on earth: "Whosoever will save his life shall lose it: and whosoever will lose his life for my sake shall find it" (Matt. 16:25).

PERGAMOS:
A COMPROMISING CHURCH

About fifteen miles from the coast of the Aegean
Sea and sixty miles north of Smyrna stands a small
Turkish town called Bergma. Its name identifies it
correctly as the site of the ancient city of Pergamos.
At the time of John's writing, Pergamos had been a
capital city for over three hundred years. Before
the Christian era it was the chief city of the At-
talid kingdom. A series of kings known as the Attalids
built Pergamos into a beautiful and imposing city. In
133 B.C. Attalis III willed his kingdom to the Romans,
who accepted the gift and made Pergamos the capital
of the Province of Asia, a position it continued to
occupy until A.D. 130. It was not equal to Ephesus
as a center of trade but exceeded Ephesus in historical fame and political importance. Pliny, the Roman
writer, called it "by far the most famous city of Asia."[11]
Pergamos was built on a mountaintop that rose
thirteen hundred feet above the surrounding Caicus
River valley. From this vantage point the city controlled the whole valley, since a hostile army could
be seen miles away and distant caravans could be

[11]Cited in Barclay, p. 47.

observed and intercepted. Its strength as a fortress increased its importance in the affairs of the region.

Sir William Ramsay said of Pergamos:

> No city of the whole of Asia Minor—so far as I have seen, and there are few of any importance which I have not seen—possesses the same imposing and dominating aspect. It is the one city of the land which forced from me the exclamation "a royal city!" I came to it after seeing the others, and that was the impression which it produced. There is something unique and overpowering in its effect, planted as it is on its magnificent hill, standing out boldly in the level plain, and dominating the valley and the mountains on the south. Other cities of the land have splendid hills which made them into powerful fortresses in ancient time; but in them the hill is as a rule the acropolis and the city lies beneath and around or before it. But here the hill was the city proper, and the great buildings, chiefly Roman, which lie below the city, were external ornaments, lending additional beauty and stateliness to it.[12]

A visitor surveying the ruins of Pergamos today sees the remains of a beautifully situated amphitheater that seated over twenty thousand, skillfully built on the side of the mountain with a spectacular view of the valley. He also sees the ruins of a library that was second in size only to the famous one located in Alexandria, Egypt. Scholars estimate that the shelves held at least 200,000 volumes. Parchment (animal skin), the material on which many of the copies of the Bible were written, was invented by these people. The name comes from the name of the city, "the Pergamene sheet." On this fact hangs a tale. There was a king of Pergamos, Eumenes, who tried to hire the chief librarian of Alexandria to come to work for him. This angered the king of Egypt, and he put his librarian in prison to make sure that he would not take advantage of the offer.

[12]Ramsay, p. 295.

Then he placed an embargo on papyrus, the main writing material of the day, made from reeds that grew along the banks of the Nile, and would not permit any to be sent to Pergamos. Since Egypt had a virtual monopoly on the production of papyrus, Pergamos was left without any writing material. In the emergency they sought a substitute, and their necessity proved the mother of invention: they discovered the suitability of animal skins for writing material.

There were three major religions in Pergamos. First, reflecting their Anatolian heritage, was the worship of Asklepios (or Aesculapius), the god of healing. The temple dedicated to this god, located at the foot of the mountain, was one of the most famous hospitals of antiquity. Asklepios was usually represented with serpents near him, and his serpent-entwined staff is still used as an insignia by physicians today.

Treatment in the hospital usually followed this plan. A patient wishing to enter the hospital was first examined by the priests. Those obviously dying were refused admittance; so also were maternity cases, for a child could not be born on the sacred temple precincts. The priest explained to the patient the terms of admission, then saw to it that he received a bath and shampoo. A sacrifice was offered, followed by a lecture on the rules of the temple and the worship of the cult. After prayer and another sacrifice, the patient was left alone until night, when his bed was placed in the abaton, or ward, and gifts were placed on the small altar nearby. Healing was attributed to the god more than to the doctors. During the night the god would appear in a dream and tell what medicines to use or, on special occasions, would come himself and operate. During the night the priest would come and collect the gifts left upon the altar. Strangely, healing often depended upon the size of the contribution made!

Treatment was a combination of medicine, psychology, and superstition. The doctors used exercise, massage, diet, rest, sun baths, mineral baths, herbs, and purgatives. They also used tame snakes to lick the spot where the patient was afflicted. For the people who had to remain for some length of time, there was diversion by music, art, theater, and religious services. Amid the ruins there is a restored odeon, or music hall, which is presently being used for performances. Since Luke joined Paul on his second journey at Troas, not far from Pergamos, it is possible that he was living in this area and in all likelihood had practiced in this very hospital.

Second, there was the worship of the Greek god Zeus. The major discovery among the ruins of the city was the remains of a huge and elaborate temple and altar dedicated to the worship of Zeus. Pergamos was excavated and studied by German archaeologists, and much that was found was taken to Germany. In the Berlin Museum today is a beautiful reconstruction of the altar, the focal point of the worship. Inscriptions have been found referring to the god as Zeus *soter* (Zeus savior).

Third, there was a Roman religion, emperor worship. As the capital of the province, Pergamos boasted the largest and most important temple dedicated to Caesar. In fact, there were three temples in the city: one dedicated to Augustus, one to Trajan, and one to Severus. Pergamos was known as keeper of Caesar's temple, as Ephesus was of the temple of Artemis (Acts 19:35).

The message to the church at Pergamos begins on an ominous note. "These things saith he which hath the sharp sword with two edges" (2:12). The sword is an emblem of war and judgment. The Lord is displeased with something about this church and is threatening to chastise it. The reference to a sword was appropriate to Pergamos, the seat of Roman authority. To the Romans the sword was the symbol of authority, carrying the power of life and death.

The Attitude of the World

"I know ... where thou dwellest, even where Satan's seat is" (2:13). The Christians at Pergamos lived among enemies of the gospel. The word translated "seat" in the King James Version is *thronos,* throne. Satan is on earth, and he has certain headquarters for his operations. In what sense was Pergamos the throne of Satan? Three answers have been given. Satan's throne may refer to the worship of Asklepios, the god of healing. He was called "savior." His symbol, the serpent, which appears on many artifacts, is one of the names of the devil. Second, the phrase may refer to the huge, magnificent altar where Zeus was worshiped as savior high on the hill of the acropolis. Third, it may refer to the Caesar worship. Any of the three kinds of idolatry would have deserved the ascription "Satan's throne," a place where Satan has special authority and power; and three together certainly made the city a stronghold of Satan.

The word "dwell," *katoikeo,* indicates a permanent dwelling place rather than a temporary one, for which the word would have been *paroikeo* (see Heb. 11:9 for the contrast in these two words). The church lived in Pergamos. It could not move away to escape persecution. God had placed the church there, and there it must stay. In life we cannot run from difficulty. Christians often find themselves in unfavorable circumstances. Business associates are wicked and profane; family members are unsaved and unsympathetic to their faith; friends of long-standing oppose and misunderstand them. Beleaguered Christians can gain help from this message to the believers of Pergamos. The Lord knew that they were in this difficult place, for He had put them there. The greater the darkness, the greater the need for a light. Soldiers must often serve in isolated, difficult places. Just as God needed a witness in Pergamos, He needs witnesses in difficult places today. Because He knows the place is hard, the

Lord can sympathize with their trials but not excuse their failures. Those who fail amidst difficulties will be judged leniently; but, if found unfaithful, they will be condemned.

The Attitude of the Church

The attitude of the church is described by the Lord as a divided, double-minded one. There is both consistency and compromise, faithfulness and tolerance. This self-contradiction is to be expected. Any church or Christian that compromises with evil must have some good qualities or there would be nothing to compromise.

Consistency toward Christ. "Thou holdest fast my name, and hast not denied my faith, even in those days wherein Antipas was my faithful martyr, who was slain among you, where Satan dwelleth" (2:13). Undergoing persecution the church had remained true. It was holding on (present tense, implying continual action) to the name of Christ. In holding on to the name of Christ, it was holding on to Christ Himself, for the name represents the person: "The name of the Lord is a strong tower: the righteous runneth into it, and is safe" (Prov. 18:10). Advocates of emperor worship could not shake these believers loose from Christ. Even in the special time of testing when one of their number, Antipas, was killed, they did not deny the faith. The Lord graciously gives to him the title ("my faithful martyr," *ho martus ho pistos*) He uses for Himself in Revelation 1:5. Originally no thought of death was connected with the word *martyr*. Because Antipas was a faithful martyr (witness), he was killed. Later the word acquired the meaning it possesses today: a person who seals his witness with his death.

Antipas preferred death to denying Christ. Others might consider him mad to throw away his life for something so apparently trivial. Why not exercise a little moderation? Why not yield a little and continue to live? But surely when Antipas awoke in the presence of his Lord he did not regret his choice. He was not the loser for his faithfulness. Why then should we fear and trim our way in order to gain the approval of a wicked world? When a man joins an army, he understands that he may have to lose his life. One who is unwilling to die in battle for his country will never make much of a soldier. We sing "Onward, Christian Soldiers," but are we willing to give up our lives for Christ? Would we be faithful unto death?

This church had much to commend it. In comparison with the number of churches and even whole denominations today that have sold out Christ and denied not only His name but also His deity, virgin birth, bodily resurrection, and power to save, this church seems great. If today's churches were threatened with what it faced, many would empty rapidly, and many who profess to be Christians would quickly renounce their past profession to gain peace and freedom from danger. This church had seen one of its members killed for no crime except that of worshiping the Lord Jesus, and yet it was holding fast.

How does one deny the faith under conditions such as those at Pergamos? First of all, by not confessing it. By keeping quiet. When the pressure came to profess loyalty to the emperor or to Asklepios, some might quietly have complied with no mention of their Christian faith. When their business declined and they could not make ends meet because of their faith in Christ, some might have given in. "After all," they could argue, "we have to live." The Christians at Pergamos, however, would not do so. They would starve before they would deny Christ. They took seriously the words of Christ, "Whosoever therefore shall confess me before men, him will I confess also before my Father which is in heaven. But whosoever shall deny me before men, him will I also deny before my Father which is in heaven" (Matt. 10:32).

Compromise with evil. In Smyrna there was a synagogue of Satan; in Pergamos there was the throne of Satan. In Smyrna the devil worked through a Jewish facade of religion; in Pergamos he was in complete control and worked boldly in the open. The great danger in a situation like Pergamos's is that the church will be pressured into forming some kind of an alliance with the forces of the enemy. The invitation to ungodly alliances is the essence of the temptation with which Satan assaulted Christ when he offered Him all the kingdoms of the world if He would worship him. Satan had tried persecution, but it had failed to shake the Christians from their firm hold on Christ. Now he came in a different guise, flattering them with worldly friendships, wealth, and pleasure.

Although the Christians at Pergamos refused steadfastly to give up Christianity for emperor worship or Zeus worship or recognition of the serpent god, Asklepios, there was something wrong: it was permitting people in the church who held to false teachings. Sound themselves, they were soft and compromising toward those who were not. The church lacked discipline. It was the leaders' responsibility to see that people who embraced error were put out of the church before they could damage others. Expulsion is not pleasant, but to fail to do it is to countenance sin. Being grieved or disapproving is not enough. There must be positive action against the offenders. Because the Lord seems gentle in His approach, we must not think that the sins were minor or unimportant. It is because they were so serious that He approaches so gently to try to win the offenders back to the proper life.

The Lord makes a distinction between the church and the members of the church. "I have a few things against *thee* [the church], because thou hast there *them* [some people in the church]" (2:14). "I will come unto *thee* [the church] quickly, and will fight against *them* [the individuals who were in error]" (2:16). The Lord mentions two groups in the church at Pergamos that had no business being there: those who held to the doctrine of Balaam and those who held to the doctrine of the Nicolaitans (2:14-15). Balaam was a strange figure who appears unannounced in the Biblical account of the Israelites' nearing the promised land (Num. 22-25). He had from God the gift of pronouncing a curse or a blessing upon people and had won considerable fame because of his power. Though he seems not to have been a saved man (his conduct and especially his end suggest he was not), he evidently had a real contact with the true God. Prophecy is a gift and not a grace. The Lord speaks of some who will say in the day of judgment, "Lord, Lord, have we not prophesied in thy name? And in thy name ... done many wonderful works?" The Lord's answer is, "I never knew you: depart from me, ye that work iniquity" (Matt. 7:22-23). Today even unregenerate Roman Catholics and liberals are claiming various gifts of the Spirit. The fact that they seem to possess some power or gift is no proof in itself that they are spiritual or even regenerated.

As the Israelites entered the land of Moab, Balak, the king, anxious lest they overrun his country, hired Balaam to curse them for him. When Balaam attempted to pronounce the curse, God permitted him to utter only blessings. II Peter refers to the "way of Balaam," who "loved the wages of unrighteousness" (2:15). This way is using the gift of God for one's own profit. Balaam was more interested in pleasing Balak, who was paying him a large sum of money, than in pleasing God who gave him the gift. When he found that he could not curse the Israelites because they were pleasing to God, he decided to corrupt them. He told Balak that if his people would intermarry with the Israelites, God would be displeased with them and destroy them Himself (Num. 31:16). Balaam thus taught Israel to "eat things sacrificed unto idols, and to commit fornication" (2:14). In the church at Pergamos, some professing Christians were teaching that these sins could be committed with impunity. They taught a carelessness or indifference toward believers' conduct. Believers, they said, could worship Christ and conform to the standards of the world.

The early believer lived in a completely pagan environment as a misfit, a gear that did not mesh with the ordinary life of the community. The temptation "to eat things sacrificed to idols" was a constant problem. A sacrifice made in the pagan temples was not completely burned up; only a very small part of the animal was given to the flames. The rest was divided between the priest and the offerer, who used his part to provide a feast for his family and friends either in his home or in the heathen temple. These Balaamites taught that it was permissible for Christians to participate in these feasts. Could they not eat meat and drink wine dedicated to the gods and enjoy some of the pleasures of their society without lending their hearts to what they knew to be a lie and a deception? This right they proclaimed as their Christian liberty. But they perverted the teaching of Paul[13] and turned Christian liberty into license. The Christian does, it is true, have liberty, but he cannot do what he likes. He must do what God likes.

[13]About four decades earlier, the Apostle Paul had written to the Corinthians about the problem of meat that is sacrificed to idols (I Cor. 8 and 10). He made the point that, in reality, an idol is nothing and that the food, therefore, is perfectly good and legitimate to eat. However, there was a question of one's Christian testimony, and, for this reason, a person should not eat if it would offend his brothers. He said that it is legitimate to eat without question what is put before you. However, if the issue be raised and it be pointed out that this is meat offered to idols, then it should not be eaten for the sake of the weak brother. John, writing to the church in a later period, does not make any reference to this permission but simply issues a blanket condemnation of the groups who taught that it is permissible to eat meat that is known to have been offered to idols.

To dine with a neighbor was to share an offering to his gods. To serve in the army required attendance at pagan ceremonies. To hold office entailed participation in the dedication of buildings and games where pagan deities were honored. These Balaamites advocated some sort of compromise that would permit being Christians and citizens of the world at the same time. Some decades before John wrote this letter to Pergamos, the Jerusalem church had taken a stand on these matters: "It seemed good to the Holy Ghost, and to us, to lay upon you no greater burden than these necessary things, that ye abstain from meats offered to idols, and from blood, and from things strangled, and from fornication: from which if ye keep yourselves, ye shall do well" (Acts 15:28-29). Paul had dealt with the problem in I Corinthians 8:13: "If meat make my brother to offend, I will eat no flesh while the world standeth." If the church had given in to those who taught and practiced such compromise, the world would soon have swallowed it up. The church cannot afford the slightest compromise with sin and paganism. The only answer that can be given to this suggestion is a strong "No." The Christian cannot eat a meal commemorating the Lord's death in church on Sunday and eat a meal in honor of a false god in a pagan temple on Monday. The Christian must remain separate and distinct from the unchristian world around him even though it costs him his friends, his job, or his life.

The Balaamites, like their namesake, were teaching God's people "to commit fornication" (2:14). As wicked as the world is today with its preference of the permissive new morality to the moral standards of the Bible, it is still difficult for us to envision the corruption of the world of John's day. The Greeks and Romans were not brought up on the teachings of the Old Testament; many had never even heard of the Hebrew Scriptures. The moral conditions in Asia at this time were like those of Burma described by Kipling in "The Road to Mandalay": "Ship me somewheres east of Suez, where the best is like the worst, Where they arn't no Ten Commandments, an' a man can raise a thirst." As far as Asia knew, there were no Ten Commandments. Prohibitions against immorality were unknown. They had never heard "Thou shalt not commit adultery." In fact, prostitution was a part of the worship in the pagan temples. Demosthenes, the famous Greek orator, accepted prostitution as part of normal existence:

> We have courtesans for the sake of pleasure; we have concubines for the sake of daily cohabitation; we have wives for the purpose of having children legitimately, and of having a faithful guardian of our household affairs.[14]

Cicero, the Roman orator and moral philosopher, defended the practice:

> If there is anyone who thinks that young men should be absolutely forbidden the love of courtesans, he is extremely severe. I am not able to deny the principle that he states. But he is at variance, not only with the licence of what our own age allows, but also with the customs and concessions of our ancestors. When indeed was this not done? When did anyone ever find fault with it? When was it that that which is now lawful was not lawful?[15]

These writers were not rebels against the society of their day; they were not trying to shock anyone. They simply expressed the moral attitudes that prevailed in their time. Into this climate came Christianity, teaching chastity and purity. The church insisted that its members no longer live as the typical gentile lived but conform to the teachings of Christ. Those holding to the doctrine of Balaam, who were encouraging Christians to commit fornication, were simply urging them

[14]Cited in Barclay, p. 60.

[15]*Ibid.*

to conform to the moral standards of the day and stop being different from their neighbors.

The second group tolerated by the church was similar. "So hast thou also them that hold the doctrine of the Nicolaitanes, which thing I hate" (2:15). In the letter to the church at Ephesus, the Lord said, "But this thou hast, that thou hatest the deeds of the Nicolaitanes, which I also hate" (2:6). What was described as deeds in Ephesus had settled into doctrines in Pergamos. What the Ephesian church hated as deeds the Pergaman church allowed as doctrine. However, since the Nicolaitans are mentioned separately from the followers of Balaam, there must have been some difference between the two groups. Little or nothing is known about the Nicolaitans, but from some allusions to them by early writers, implying that they tolerated sin in the church, most commentators today believe they were similar to the Balaamites but more open in introducing pagan practices into the church.

The Lord knew that if this compromise were allowed, the church eventually would be destroyed. Not the faintest shadow of participation in idolatry must be allowed. Even though their intentions may have been good, these men were wrong and must be opposed. It is important that we hate what Christ hates. In Malachi 2:16, for example, we learn that the Lord hates divorce. Why then should it be glossed over and condoned by His church today? What God hates we must be careful not to allow. Vance Havner has said, "You cannot be a Christian and a Balaamite. You cannot sing 'There is no other way but the way of the cross,' if you are unwilling also to sing 'Then I bid farewell to the way of the world.' You cannot take your stand 'beneath the cross of Jesus' if you are not 'content to let the world go by.' You cannot properly 'survey the wondrous cross' and not sacrifice 'the vain things that charm you most' to His blood. You cannot sing 'My Jesus, I love Thee' and mean it until for Him 'all the follies of sin' you resign. You cannot sing from your heart 'whiter than snow' if you are unwilling for the Lord to 'break down every idol, cast out every foe.'"[16] It is not possible to serve two masters. We must be all out for Christ, or we will end up serving Satan. "Wherefore come out from among them, and be ye separate, saith the Lord, and touch not the unclean thing; and I will receive you" (II Cor. 6:17).

The Attitude of the Lord

Repentance for sin. "Repent; or else I will come unto thee quickly, and will fight against them with the sword of my mouth" (2:16). The Balaamites and Nicolaitans may have felt they were secure in the soft, compromising attitude of the church, not realizing they would have to face the sharp sword of the Lord. If the church would not take action, the Lord Himself would intervene. It is interesting that the original Balaam perished by the sword (Num. 31:8). Controversy or battle is not the bane of the church but its salvation. To repent is to change one's attitude and to show that change by a different conduct. If a church repents, there will be conflict. The evil ones must be expelled for the purity of the church to be restored. But the church that refuses to battle evil accepts battle with God. Christ will always forgive past indifference and failure if there is genuine repentance and endeavor for new obedience. No one is so far gone that he will not find a welcome and forgiveness if he will only seek the Lord in confession and determination to live for Him.

Reward for overcomers. Some members did not concur in the general attitude of the church toward evil; they did not endorse the compromise of the church as a whole. Christ promises them a reward. "To him

[16]Havner, p. 46.

that overcometh will I give to eat of the hidden
manna" (2:17). To those who steadfastly refused the
enticements of the world to eat idol sacrifices, He offers
the bread of God, "The hidden manna" (2:17). Manna
fed the children of Israel in the wilderness as they
journeyed toward the promised land. But that mirac-
ulous bread was a type of a yet better food. The Saviour
said, "I am the living bread which came down from
heaven" (John 6:51). Christ Himself is the nourishment
and strength of the Christian. But the promise for
overcomers is for the future: "I *will* give to eat." In
heaven the Christian will be rewarded by fellowship
with His Lord and, even there, will be sustained and
cared for by Him.

But there is more: "and will give him a white stone,
and in the stone a new name written, which no man
knoweth saving he that receiveth it" (2:17). The
significance of the white stone is not known. Commentators have ventured several guesses based on what we
know of the customs of those times. One popular view
is that the reference was to a ballot. In ancient times
votes were taken by the placing of stones in a vessel.
A black stone was an unfavorable vote and a white
stone was a vote for acceptance. Today we speak of
blacklisting or blackballing someone for an offense.
The gift of the white stone may mean that when a man
is faithful to God, God will acquit him. Some base their
interpretation on the use of stones for admission tickets
to games and sporting events.

According to another view, the white stone is an
emblem of victory and, hence, indicates a memorable
occasion. Pliny speaks of a day "marked by the whitest
of white stones,"[17] just as we refer to a "red letter day."
Still another view is that the reference was to amulets
often worn in those times as a protection against evil.
These were made of precious metals or white stones

[17]Cited in Barclay, p. 62.

with some mystical writing on them to make them effective. Christians have no need of these. God is the protection of the Christian, and His name is written on their hearts just as their names are written on His hands.

Some writers think that the stone is a reference to the urim, the stone worn by the high priest, probably a diamond. Just as by means of a white stone the Israelites found the will of God, so the overcomer is made a priest and enjoys fellowship and the knowledge of God. Just as Phineas was promised an everlasting priesthood for his loyalty to God in opposing Balaam (Num. 24:11-13), so these first-century Christians who opposed Balaamism are designated a priesthood.

In any case, the Lord takes an object familiar to the people and gives it a new significance. The giving of a new name, the name of the Lord, alludes to the practice by some mystery religions of giving their members secret names for their protection and help. Ramsay suggests that in a town that was a center of Roman administration, the new name would have had a veiled reference of opposition to emperor worship under the name of Augustus that was assumed by each of the emperors. He also cites an interesting reference to an orator who received a new name from the serpent god Asklepios that served as a help and encouragement to him, insuring success in his work.[18]

In a hostile environment and with a compromising church, it is possible for individual Christians to remain true to Christ, resisting the evil that seeks to destroy the testimony of the church. May God grant that we will have the determination and strength to live as overcomers in our day.

[18]Ramsay, pp. 310, 312.

THYATIRA: A DIVIDED CHURCH

Thyatira was the smallest, youngest, and least important of the seven cities to which John wrote. Today it has the name Akhisar, and its population is about twenty-five thousand. It lay halfway between Pergamos and Sardis (about thirty-five to forty miles from each) and on the main highway that ran from Byzantium to Smyrna. The city was founded by Seleucius I, one of Alexander's generals and founder of the Seleucid dynasty.

Thyatira was not, like Pergamos, a natural fortress that could be easily defended. There was no nearby hill that could be fortified. But since it lay in the valley of the Caicus River, which was the natural approach to Pergamos, the capital, it did have some strategic importance. It was a pawn in the struggle between the kingdom of Pergamos and the kings of the east. It was, to use a modern term, expendable. Its function was to delay the progress of any invaders from the east until Pergamos could make the necessary preparations for defense. Captured many times and destroyed, it was always rebuilt to fight again, and it continued to prosper as an outpost town inhabited mainly by a military garrison. With the coming of the Roman peace, Thyatira was no longer needed as a military post, and it grew into a great commercial city because of its location. It was a natural stopping point for caravans traveling the important roads that passed through the city. It became a center of the wool trade, marketing a much-sought-after black wool. It also manufactured a very expensive purple dye sold all over the ancient world. Paul's first convert in Europe, Lydia, was a native of Thyatira and a seller of purple (Acts 16:14). An outstanding feature of the commercial life of Thyatira was its large number of trade guilds, organizations similar to the labor unions of today. Because of the great commercial activity, the guilds had grown very wealthy and powerful. Membership in the appropriate guild was essential for anyone who wanted to practice a craft or trade in Thyatira.

The message to Thyatira gives a picture of a divided church. The doctrinal division at Pergamos had affected conduct in Thyatira to the point of producing a sharp cleavage between those who were true to Christ and those who were deep in sin. There were the church of Jesus and the church of Jezebel. Consequently, to Thyatira the Lord appears as "the Son of God, who hath his eyes like unto a flame of fire, and his feet. . . like fine brass [bronze]" (2:18). Fire and bronze, both symbols of judgment, indicate that the Lord is displeased and that the letter will be one of rebuke and condemnation. His name, "Son of God," emphasizes that He has the power and authority to carry out the threat that He makes. The reference to might and authority would be especially significant to the inhabitants of what was originally a military town. The word translated "fine brass" (fine bronze) occurs only in the Book of Revelation. One of the trade guilds of Thyatira was of bronzesmiths and modelers in bronze. A coin from Thyatira pictures a bronzesmith. Although we do not know exactly what the term means, it is likely that this fine bronze (*chalkolibanos*) was made in the city as one of their specialities and would be familiar to them.

The Church of Jezebel

Its character. In Thyatira lived a woman the Lord calls Jezebel. This was not her real name but a portrayal of her character. The Lord is alluding to Ahab's wicked queen, a daughter of the king of Sidon, who introduced the Baal worship of her native Phoenicia into Israel and opposed the prophet Elijah. Morally and religiously she led Israel astray. The Lord used her name (the worst conceivable) to indicate the evilness of her influence at Thyatira. Women have been greatly used of God in the work of the church. Paul mentions several women who have worked with him in the gospel (Rom. 16:1-2, 6; Phil. 4:3; I Tim. 5:9-12). Often women seem more inclined to accept the gospel and serve Christ (on the mission field, for example) than men. But the same qualities that make a woman so useful in the service of Christ also make her capable of causing dissent, division, and defection from truth. Whereas Ephesus was told to do the first works, Thyatira's works were increasing. But good works do not justify false teaching. Many today would excuse a man for his errors in doctrine and practice because he is "doing so much good," but the "good" only makes his teachings more dangerous.

This Jezebel, whoever she was, called herself a prophetess. Whatever the nature of her gift, she certainly was not a prophetess of the true God. Even some of the leaders must have been deceived, for they allowed her to stay in the church. She taught the people to "commit fornication, and to eat things sacrificed unto idols" (2:20). Her teaching sounds very similar to that of the Balaamites and the Nicolaitans at Pergamos, which obliterated the distinction between Christian purity and heathen debauchery. Providing an aura of legitimacy for carnal indulgence and immorality within the church, she sanctioned sin. Is the term "to commit fornication" literal or figurative? Throughout both the Old and New Testaments, unfaithfulness to God is described as adultery. To break one's vows to God is just as base as breaking one's vows to one's marriage partner. But the licentiousness of the pagan society in New Testament times gives us reason to think that the term could very well be meant literally. We get some indication of what the prophetess was teaching from the reference in verse 24 to those "who have not known the depths [deep things] of Satan, as they speak." She was teaching some "deep" esoteric philosophy that issued in immorality and came from the devil. Any philosophy that makes it easier to sin is of the devil.

Barclay suggests that her teaching was motivated by the circumstance of the many strong trade guilds that controlled manufacturing and selling. A businessman could not prosper without belonging to one of them. A man who refused to join his guild would be in much the same position as a man in one of our northern industrial cities who refused to join a union: he could not work. But why would these Christians refuse to join one of the guilds? What could be wrong with belonging to a trade union? The answer is found in the fact that these guilds, like unions and civic clubs today, had certain social activities, and these activities were closely connected with the worship of pagan gods. The meals included invocations to the gods. They began and ended with a libation to the gods. The meat was usually from a sacrifice. Often the celebrations degenerated into drunken orgies. What were these Christians to do? They must live; they had families to support. No one likes to be despised and ostracized by his neighbors. T. R. Glover cites Tertullian on this question: "There [*On Idolatry*] he deals with Christians who earn their living by making idols—statuaries, painters, guilders, and the like; and when the plea is suggested that they *must* live and have no other way of living, he indignantly retorts that they should have thought this out before. *Vivere ergo habes? Must* you live? he asks. Elsewhere he says, 'there are no *musts* where faith is concerned.'"[19] Faithful Christians rightly felt that they could not participate in such activities. How could they partake of both the Lord's cup and the cup of demons (I Cor. 10:21)? They knew the church must remain separate from the pagan world or be swallowed by it. But this woman, Jezebel, was teaching that Christians could become members of the trade guilds, attending the heathen ceremonies and compromising in idolatrous practices, in order to protect their business interests. When business requires practices contrary to the principles of the Scriptures, what must the Christian do? When society urges and endorses mores not compatible with Christian standards, what must the individual do? Which is more important, our business or our relation to Christ?

This false teaching had been going on for some time. The Lord had given her "space to repent of her fornication; and she repented not" (2:21). The Lord is long-suffering, not eager to punish but desirous that men repent. However, His patience is not unlimited. He spared the Amorites for four hundred years but finally destroyed them (Gen. 15:13-16). In Israel's history, after generations of disobedience, God's patience finally was exhausted and judgment came. Christ said of Jerusalem, "How often would I have gathered thy children together, even as a hen gathereth her chickens under her wings, and ye would not! Behold, your house is left unto you desolate" (Matt. 23:37-38). Now the time of judgment for the church at Thyatira was at hand.

Its condemnation. "Behold I will cast her into a bed, and them that commit adultery with her into great

[19]Cited in T. R. Glover, *Conflicts of Religion in the Early Roman Empire* (London: Methuen, 1909), p. 321.

tribulation, except they repent of their deeds. And I will kill her children with death" (2:22-23). Punishment is mentioned separately for Jezebel, the leader, and her children, the followers. Jezebel will be thrown into a bed. The word "bed" (*kline*) is used of a banquet couch as well as of a bed for sleeping, and one possible interpretation is that just as she urged Christians to recline at pagan banquets so she would be struck down while at one of these feasts. Since respectable women did not eat with the men at their feasts, the condemnation, if this explanation is correct, shows what sort of woman she was. Seiss argues from Psalm 139:8 ("if I make my bed in hell") that her destiny is hell. Others associate the bed with her adulterous acts. Since a bed was involved in her sin, she is fittingly cast into a bed of punishment, into great tribulation.

Her disciples also will be punished with death. They will be cut off in such a sudden and unexpected way that "all the churches shall know that I am he which searcheth the reins [minds] and hearts" (2:23). It will be evident to all that God has judged the wicked. Nothing in our intellectual or emotional life can be hidden from Him (Heb. 4:13).

Even at this late hour the offer to escape judgment is still extended: "Except they repent of their deeds" (2:22). God declares, "I have no pleasure in the death of the wicked; but that the wicked turn from his way and live" (Ezek. 33:11). Today God, as in John's day, offers forgiveness of sin and salvation to all who will repent of their sins and turn in faith to Him.

The Church of Jesus

Very few churches become completely apostate. No matter how far a church may depart from the truth, it usually has among its members some children of God. In the letter to Thyatira, the Lord addresses His words not to the intruders, the false teachers, but to His people.

Its endeavors. "I know thy works, and charity, and service, and faith, and thy patience, and thy works: and the last to be more than the first" (2:19). The church at Thyatira served God, had faith, patiently endured opposition, and persevered in good works. Two pairs of virtues are mentioned: love and service; faith and patience. Love for Christ is always manifested in service. When we love someone, we want to give to him and work for him. The person who sings "O How I Love Jesus" and makes no effort to serve Him has very little love in his heart. The proof of love is service. Likewise, one who has faith in Christ, true saving faith implanted by the Holy Spirit, will be ready to endure for Christ's sake whatever suffering, hardship, or ridicule this Satan-controlled world may bring to him. Patience means perseverance, not becoming discouraged and giving up in the face of opposition. The proof of faith is endurance. All of these virtues the church had. Not only did they exist, but they were increasing: "the last" were "more than the first." In spite of adversity (or perhaps because of it) they were growing. Growth is a good sign; we must ever seek to grow in grace. As soon as we cease to grow, we begin to decline. Neither churches nor individuals can afford to rest on their past achievements. They must constantly press toward new goals. As the songwriter says, "My prayer, my aim is higher ground."

Its indifference. "Notwithstanding, I have a few things against thee, because thou sufferest that woman Jezebel" (2:20). The Ephesians were orthodox and vigilant against false doctrine, but they had left their first love. The Christians of Thyatira had love but were so sweet and pleasant that they tolerated everything including Jezebel and her teaching. The church of Thyatira, like that of Pergamos, sinned in permitting evil. The charge that it permitted evil implies that it could have forced the evil out if it had wanted to. It

is not unchristian to oppose heresy; it is unchristian
not to oppose it. The letter first condemns the leader;
it is his fault. It also, however, blames the officers and
members for not taking action. False teaching never
goes away of its own accord. Furthermore, it is never
willing to coexist with the truth. Any pretense at
coexistence is always for the ultimate purpose of
destroying truth and taking absolute control. Just as
communism will not willingly coexist with the free
world, so it is impossible for the church to tolerate
error in its membership. Error *will not* coexist with
truth, and, therefore, truth *cannot* coexist with error.
The only alternatives are the conversion of the false
teacher or his expulsion. In America in this century,
the major denominations were infiltrated by men who
openly taught doctrines contrary to the Scriptures as
well as to their creeds. From seminary classrooms and
pulpits they infected prospective ministers and church
members with their false teachings. Incredibly, they
were permitted to remain. They were regarded as
"Christian brothers" who differed on some matters of
interpretation but were entirely within their rights to
do so. As a result whole denominations have fallen into
their hands, and under their control the Bible-believers
have been silenced or forced out. The church at Thyatira had not yet reached this stage. God did not tell the
faithful group to get out. The evil one could be expelled
if the church would obey the warning and take action
If they would not, God would step in and judge them.

Its triumph. "But unto you I say, and unto the rest
in Thyatira, as many as have not this doctrine" (2:24).
In Thyatira there was a remnant, a group that had not
followed Jezebel and her licentious practices. They had
not accepted her teaching, had not known the "depths
of Satan." With this group, probably hard pressed and
persecuted, the Lord deals gently and graciously. All

He asks is that they hold on to what they have until He returns. What did these Christians have to hold on to? Not much perhaps in material goods, but they had faith in Christ. They had the gospel with all of its comforts and enablements. They had Christ Himself as Protector and Friend and Companion. Oh, that Christians today would realize the greatness of these possessions and hold fast, not in their own strength but "in the strength which God supplies through His eternal Son" (Charles Wesley).

"Till I come" (2:25). Here the message transcends the local church at Thyatira, including the church of all ages everywhere. The exhortation is, "He that hath an ear, let him hear what the Spirit saith unto the *churches* [note the plural]" (2:29). The Christians at Thyatira were to look for and expect the soon coming of the Lord. But all Christians today can receive the same message with perfect appropriateness. "Hold fast till I come" is the hope of the church today just as when John wrote.

To the faithful in Thyatira two promises were given: "And he that overcometh, and keepeth my works unto the end, to him will I give power over the nations: and he shall rule them with a rod of iron; as the vessels of a potter shall they be broken to shivers: even as I received of my Father. And I will give him the morning star" (2:26-28). One of the characteristics of the true Christian is that he perseveres. Saving faith is permanent and lasting; otherwise it does not really save. Who wants a temporary salvation that does not get its possessor to heaven? These overcoming Christians were to keep the Lord's works to the end. The Christian life is not a battle but a war, a lifelong struggle against the world and the devil. The letter contrasts "their deeds" (or, as some translate it, "her works"), verse 22, and "my works, " verse 26. We must choose whom we are going to obey. Victory is promised us. We dare not give up. "Ne'er think the vict'ry won, nor lay thine

armor down; The work of faith will not be done till
thou obtain the crown" (George Heath).

These Christians were promised a rule over the
nations. These poor, despised people, "of whom the
world was not worthy" (Heb. 11:38), were to become
the lords of the earth. The Philadelphian church was
promised that those who hated and opposed them
would have to come and worship before their feet (3:9).
So it was with Thyatira. The rule of the saints is a
theme running through the Scriptures. "But the saints
of the most High shall take the kingdom, and possess
the kingdom forever. And the kingdom and dominion,
and the greatness of the kingdom under the whole heav-
en, shall be given to the people of the saints of the
Most High" (Dan. 7:18, 27). "Ye which have followed
me, in the regeneration, when the Son of Man shall sit
in the throne of his glory, ye also shall sit upon twelve
thrones, judging the twelve tribes of Israel" (Matt.
19:28). "Do ye not know that the saints shall judge the
world?" (I Cor. 6:3). The fulfillment of this promise of
rule will come after the Lord has returned to earth and
established His kingdom in righteousness. The promise
in verses 26 and 27 refers to the second Psalm, in
which God backs by oath His solemn promise that His
Son, the Messiah, will rule the nations. This promise
Christ will share with the church just as He shares
with His joint heirs so much else that belongs to Him
(Rom. 8:17).

The second promise is, "I will give him the morning
star" (2:28). This gift consists of Christ Himself. "I am
the root and the offspring of David, and the bright and
morning star" (Rev. 22:16). After Christ returns, after
His kingdom is set up, while we rule with Him over the
nations, our most precious possession will still be
Christ Himself. "Unto you therefore which believe he
is precious" (I Pet. 2:7). "Whom having not seen, ye
love" (I Pet. 1:8).

While we wait for that glorious day the church must

be vigilant. The call of the New Testament is for the church to separate from evil. Jezebel is being tolerated today, and she must be opposed. We, like the saints at Thyatira, must fight to keep the Lord's works to the end and defend the "faith which was once delivered unto the saints" (Jude 3).

Leave no unguarded place, no weakness of the soul,
  Take every virtue, every grace, and fortify the whole.
From strength to strength go on, wrestle and fight and pray,
  Tread all the powers of darkness down, and win the well-fought day.

SARDIS: A LIFELESS CHURCH

We must not forget that the letters our Lord wrote to the seven churches were addressed to actual churches. The cities where they resided were actual cities. They had buildings; they had citizens; they had problems just as our cities do today. Each city had its history, its importance, its individuality. Often the church reflected some of the characteristics of the city where it was located.

Sardis was an old and famous city. Its history reached back twelve hundred years before Christ. Located about fifty miles inland from the Aegean Sea, almost due east of the city of Smyrna (modern Izmir), it lay in a valley formed by the convergence of two rivers. For many centuries it was a well-populated center of trade. In addition to the city that lay in the valley, a second city was built upon nearby Mount Tmolus, rising with sheer sides about fifteen hundred feet above the valley. There Sardis built its acropolis, an impregnable fortress for defense against attack, and a means of controlling commerce through the valley. In ancient times Sardis profited from a tariff imposed on caravans passing through their valley.

Long before the Book of Revelation was written, the city of Sardis was the capital of the Lydian Kingdom.

Solon, the great Greek legislator, lived in Sardis for a while. Thales, the father of Greek philosophy, was a native of the city. Its most famous king was Cresus, whose name even today, in the saying "as rich as Cresus," designates a very wealthy man.

Sardis was a great center of trade and commerce. It sat like the hub of a wheel at the intersection of great highways reaching out in all directions, one going southwest to Ephesus, one northwest toward Thyatira and Pergamos, another east into the interior of Anatolia or central Turkey, and another southeast toward the city of Laodicea. Up and down these highways moved the trade of ancient times. This area was the connecting link between the east and the west, between the oriental nations and those of Greece and Rome. When the Persian Empire came into power, the Lydian Kingdom fell and Sardis became a vassal of the Persians. Nevertheless, it continued to prosper, not only under Persian rule but also under the dominion of Greece and Rome.

In the year A.D. 17 a great earthquake shook the region and completely destroyed the city. The Roman emperor Tiberius made a special concession to Sardis, waiving taxation for five years and sending over a quarter of a million dollars to help in the rebuilding of the city. Coins have been found commemorating Caesar's benevolence. Sardis recovered from this disaster quickly and again became a wealthy city. In earlier times the river Pactolus that ran through the city contained gold, furnishing the city with readily available wealth. Cresus, its best-known king, is credited with being the first to coin money out of bullion.

Sardis was also a religious city. In the ruins today stands a huge temple originally thought to have been dedicated to the worship of Artemis. Because of the nature of this worship, Sardis was also a wicked city. Through the centuries it was known for the loose living of its people. As part of the Roman Empire the city had peace; armies no longer marched up and down the valley seeking conquest. Gradually the acropolis became uninhabited and fell into decay, remaining so until the wars of the Turkish period centuries later. As peace brought greater prosperity to the city, it became more and more decadent, more and more indifferent to moral values. It began to be looked upon with contempt. Cyrus had forced the Lydians to give up their warlike habits and to teach their children to use musical instruments instead of weapons. His decree had changed their whole manner of life. The city remained peaceful and prosperous, but it was dying. Outwardly vigorous and active, it contained the seeds of decay and death. Whereas Smyrna was dead and yet living, Sardis was living and yet dead.

The Condemnation

The letter to Sardis is a message of condemnation. Most of the letters to the churches begin by enumerating some good points of the church; but in the case of Sardis, there is nothing good to be said, only condemnation. There is some similarity between the accounts of this church and of Ephesus. Both were deteriorating, but Ephesus had not gone so far as Sardis. To Ephesus Christ appeared as the One who "holdeth the seven stars in his right hand, who walketh in the midst of the seven golden candlesticks" (2:1); to Sardis, "He that hath the seven Spirits of God, and the seven stars" (3:1). In both, Christ is pictured as the center of the church. The Spirit is described as "seven Spirits" because He is working in each of the seven churches. "I know thy works, that thou hast a name that thou livest, and art dead" (3:1). The church was like the city: apparently alive but actually dead. Outwardly the church was still prosperous—it had a name to be alive—but spiritually it was dead. It seems to have been untroubled by Jewish persecution, pressure from the cult of emperor worship, and internal heresies that disturbed the other churches. Outwardly all was well. The services were being held regularly; attendance was steady. Spiritually, however, it was dead.

What are the signs of a dying church? A church is in danger of dying when it begins to tolerate those who wish to turn it from the Scriptures. A church that is still sound, that is still preaching the gospel, that has Bible-believing members may for some reason or another begin to accept those who deny the inspiration of the Scriptures, the deity of Christ, and the necessity of salvation. It no longer wants to take scriptural positions that will cause it to be looked upon as odd. It cooperates with and acknowledges as Christians those who differ with it on the great doctrines of the Scriptures. The church then is in danger of dying.

A church is in danger of dying when it becomes more interested in external things than in spiritual things. For some churches the material is everything. The people want a more beautiful building, a bigger organ, better equipment, and more members. They want to baptize more people, not as a result of winning them to Christ but for the sake of a better report. When a church becomes more of a social club than a place for promoting the gospel, when it is more interested in being acceptable to other churches than in being acceptable to the Head of the church, that church is in danger of dying.

A church is in danger of dying when it is satisfied with its present condition. Some churches are perfectly content with themselves. There can be nothing wrong with them. Anyone who does not completely agree with them is either a fanatic or a compromiser. No matter how the attendance falls off and the membership dwindles, they are satisfied. Nothing must be changed; nothing must be altered in any way. There is something wrong with everyone else but not with them. As the members sit Sunday after Sunday enjoying the services, they blame all their misfortunes on external causes instead of on themselves. Such a church is in danger of dying.

What are the signs of a living church? The first is growth. If a child does not grow, there is something wrong physically. Likewise, a church that is not growing has something wrong with it spiritually. The lives of the individual members should exhibit growth. There should be growth in missionary activity, in giving, in attendance and membership. Growth indicates life.

Second, a church that is alive is a church with compassion. Compassion is related to growth, for it motivates evangelism. A living church has a desire to win the lost to Jesus Christ: the poor and needy as well as the rich and sophisticated. A church that is alive has some emotion in it. As individuals we laugh, we cry, we rejoice, we mourn. We have feeling. A church that has no feeling is a church that is almost dead.

The Command

In the second verse the Lord commands, "Be watchful, and strengthen the things which remain, that are ready to die: for I have not found thy works perfect before God." The word translated "Be watchful" (*gregoreo*) literally means "wake up." In the garden of Gethsemane when Christ returned from praying and found His disciples asleep, He awoke them saying, "Could ye not watch [stay awake] with me one hour?" (Matt. 26:40). At another time Jesus said, "If the good man of the house had known what hour the thief would come, he would have watched, and not have suffered his house to be broken into" (Luke 12:39). He would have sat up and lain in wait for the thief and driven him off. The Lord is telling the church at Sardis to stay awake and alert. Where should we watch? Obviously, at our weak point. Shakespeare's tragic heroes generally are destroyed at their weak point. Macbeth was ruined by ambition; Antony by lust. Bible characters are no different. Samson's weakness was women. King Saul's was pride. Everyone has a weak point at which the devil may attack. It may be a tendency to lie. The writer of Hebrews exhorts, "Lay aside every weight, and the sin which doth so easily beset us" (12:1). We need to watch at our weak point.

It is not so obvious but just as true that we need to watch at our strong point. One of Shakespeare's heroes, Othello, fell as a result of temptation at his strong point: an unjealous spirit. After his victory over the priests of Baal on Mount Carmel, Elijah succumbed to fear. Paul said, "Let him that thinketh he standeth take heed lest he fall" (I Cor. 10:12). Our strong point is sometimes the very place at which the devil will slip up on us. Herodotus, the Greek historian, tells an interesting story about Sardis that bears this out. The mythological founder of Sardis, Meles, was given the power to render the acropolis impregnable by carrying a lion all around the fortifications. Meles began his way around the walls. However, carrying a lion is something of a task. When he came to the south wall and saw how steep the mountain was at this point, he said, "Nobody can get up the mountain to attack here," and, thinking he was safe, did not carry the lion along that side of the walls. Many years went by, and the famous Lydian king, Cresus, was engaged in battle with Cyrus, the king of Persia. Cresus withdrew to his mountain fortress, confident that he could withstand the siege until the reinforcements he had sent for arrived. Cyrus looked the situation over and offered a reward to the first soldier who would climb the side of the mountain and scale the walls. The Persians, launching an attack, were driven back with large losses, whereupon they withdrew and settled into a siege of the city. One of the Persians on guard near the foot of the mountain was watching the city when a Lydian soldier on top of the wall dropped his helmet; it came clattering down the side of the mountain. As the Persian watched, the Lydian came climbing down after it. Very carefully he maneuvered down the mountain until he got the helmet and then climbed back up. The Persian reasoned that if the Lydian could scale the mountain he could also. That night he and a group of Persian soldiers followed the route the Lydian had taken to the top of the mountain and over the walls. These walls were not guarded because the slope was thought so steep that no attack could come from that side. The city fell because the occupants did not watch at their strong point. Very nearly the same thing happened about three hundred years later. A Syrian king named Antiochus III was attacking Sardis. As his men stood on guard around the foot of the mountain, one of them noticed a flock of birds sitting on the walls. He reasoned that there must not be any guards there or they would frighten the birds away. That night they went up the steep hill and over the walls, and again the city fell. Sardis had not learned the lesson of history. When the angel brought the message of God to be watchful, these Christians in Sardis must have remembered the history of their own city and the failure that had come because of a lack of watchfulness. The warning to us is to watch—at the strong point as well as at the weak point.

The church at Sardis was not only to be watchful but also to "strengthen the things which remain." A few things in Sardis had not yet completely died and could be strengthened. The church still went through the exercises of worship. They had their Sunday morning service; they took up offerings; they sang their hymns. These were good. But the life had gone out of them. The Lord does not say, "Throw all of these things away." He says, "Revitalize them. Take the things that remain and bring them back to life. Strengthen them." Once the life has gone out of a church, unless the things that remain are brought back to life or strengthened, the church itself will soon pass out of existence. At this stage of degeneration only the eagle eye of the Lord could detect that Sardis was a dead church, but if it continued much further, even its neighbors would know.

"I have not found thy works perfect before God." We come to Christ for many things—for salvation, for forgiveness of sin, for strength, for courage, for wisdom, and for comfort—and we should. All of these are necessary. One who has not yet come is without hope, for there is no true life apart from Jesus Christ. What we may fail to realize, however, is that Christ comes to us expecting something from us. We speak of the power of Christ, and yet strangely He has chosen to work through us. Christ has chosen to use human beings to accomplish His purpose. He uses the hand of the surgeon to heal the sick; the hand of the wealthy man to support His work; the hand of the minister to explain the way of life to the lost sinner. He depends on us to do His work. Christians have responsibilities to God. A poet once said:

Thou hast no hands, O Christ, as once of old
    To feed the multitudes with bread divine.
Thou hast the living bread enough for all,
    But there's no hand to give it out but mine.
Thou hast no feet, O Christ, as once to go
    Where thy lost sheep in sin and sorrow pine.
Thy love is still the same, as deep, as true,
    But thou hast no feet to go but mine.

The Cure

The cure for death is offered the church in verse 3: "Remember therefore how thou hast received and heard, and hold fast and repent." The remedy is to go back to the old ways. The verb tenses are significant in the original Greek. The verb translated "remember" is in the present tense, which in Greek expresses a continual or progressive action: "Keep on remembering" or

"Be continually remembering." The word translated "hast received" is in the perfect tense, which expresses an action that took place in the past whose effects continue to the present. In the past these Christians in Sardis had received Christ, and they still had Him. The word translated "heard" is in the aorist tense, which expresses an action that takes place at a point of time. In the indicative mood, aorist action takes place in the past. At one point of time in the past, then, the Christians of Sardis had heard about Christ and He had come into their lives. The word translated "repent" is also an aorist. It was necessary that there come a moment when this church would turn, confess its sins, forsake its deadness and whatever was hindering it, and make a new start. There must come a time in the life of everyone who is away from God when there is a change, a decision to leave sin and follow Christ, to forsake whatever is holding him back and yield completely to God. Then He says, "Hold fast." This verb is in the present tense, suggesting continual action. What a beautiful picture of the Christian life! A repentance that at one time occurs in the life and then a lifelong holding fast to Jesus Christ, the Saviour. This is the answer, this is the cure, that the Saviour proposes.

Remember, repent, hold fast. If not, He says, "I will come on thee as a thief, and thou shalt not know what hour I will come upon thee" (3:3). We often preach and think about the second coming of Christ—the blessedness of it, the glory of the time when He will come back to earth. But the second coming of Christ is not going to be an unmixed joy for everyone. A child is not eager to see his father come home from work if he has been disobedient during the day and knows that judgment comes with his father. The Apostle John says that we should so live that when Christ returns we will not be ashamed to see Him (I John 2:28). Jesus says He is coming as a thief. He will be met either with joy or with shame. The difference is the way the believer has lived.

The Lord urges these Christians in Sardis to repent, to get their lives straightened out, to come back to Him, lest He come upon them as a thief and they suffer loss.

Although there is a note of terror and warning here for the careless and indifferent, and perhaps even for the faithful, Alexander Whyte says concerning those who are true to Christ:

> Perfect love casteth out all such terror; perfect love to Christ, and to His work, and to His coming, delivers them who through fear of His coming, have all their days been subject to terror. If I love you, you cannot come too soon to me. And the more unexpected your coming is to my door the more welcome will you be to me. If I am watching and counting and keeping the hours till you come, you cannot come on me as a thief. Christ could not come on Teresa as a thief as long as she clapped her hands for His coming every time her clock struck. He cannot come too soon for me if I am always saying to myself,—why tarry the wheels of His chariot? If my last thought before I sleep is about you I will be glad to see your face and hear your voice the first thing in the morning. When I awake I am still with Thee.[20]

The Master points out, as in all of these letters, that there are a few faithful ones left. The church, He says, is dead, but a few have remained true to Christ. "Thou hast a few names even in Sardis which have not defiled their garments; and they shall walk with me in white: for they are worthy" (3:4). White was then, as now, a color of purity. Wearing white was a condition for worship among the pagans, although purity was thought of more in a ceremonial than in a moral sense. It was the custom to enter Greek temples in clean white clothing; it was a great sacrilege to enter in dirty clothes. Patients in the hospital-temple of Asculapius were fitted with white garments as soon as they arrived. Roman citizens wore white togas on holidays

[20]Alexander Whyte, *Bible Characters: Our Lord's Characters* (New York: Revell, nd), pp. 290-291.

and at religious festivals. Ramsay says, "Especially
on the day of a Triumph, white was the universal
colour—though the soldiers, of course, wore not the
toga, the garb of peace, but their full-dress military
attire with all their decorations—and there can hardly
be any doubt that the idea of walking in a Triumph
similar to that celebrated by a victorious Roman general is here present in the mind of the writer when he
uses the words, 'they shall walk with me in white.'" [21]
Paul had this Triumph in mind when he wrote to the
Colossians of the work of Christ, "He made a show of
them [principalities and powers] openly, triumphing
over them in it" (Col. 2:15). Paul saw the enemies of
Christ and of the Christians defeated and paraded in
the Triumph to glorify Christ, the Conqueror. Even
today in the territory where these churches existed, the
Moslems will ceremoniously wash their hands and feet
and faces before going into the mosque to pray. It used
to be that when we went to church we put on our "Sun-
day-go-to-meeting clothes." These were the best we had.
We wanted to honor God; and, therefore, we entered
His house wearing the best clothes we had. I have no
sympathy with people who enter God's house in sloven-
ly dress, with no attempt to make themselves present-
able. This unconcern is a sign of disrespect, of a low
view of God. We would dress up to meet the President.
How much more should we not attend to our appearance before the God of the universe?

These few in Sardis had not defiled their garments.
It is not easy to walk in the world with undefiled garments, and yet these people had done it. Before an
operation, a doctor takes great pains to cleanse himself: to scrub his hands and arms, to put on clothes that
are spotlessly clean. Contamination is all around him,
and he does not want to pass it on to the person who
is ill. Christians walk daily amidst contamination and

[21]Ramsay, p. 386.

must be careful not to defile their garments. It is possible. Joseph lived amidst the wickedness and idolatry of the court of Pharaoh, but no sin was found in him. Daniel lived in the corrupt court of Babylon but did not defile himself. It is possible to walk in a wicked world with undefiled garments.

The Culmination

The few who have kept their purity the Lord promises to reward by giving them white garments: "they shall be clothed in white raiment." These are not the same garments they had kept undefiled but a reward. He is giving them white garments to wear when they walk before Him (see 3:18; 4:4; 6:11).

The Lord also says, "I will not blot his name out of the book of life, but I will confess his name before my Father, and before the angels." The Roman church thinks it can blot a person's name out of the Book of Life. When Savonarola was excommunicated, the pope sent him a special emissary who said, "I separate thee from the church militant and from the church triumphant." Savonarola looked at him and replied, "From the church militant, yes; but from the church triumphant, never! It is not within your power to do this." Martin Luther was excommunicated from his church, consigned to damnation. But the Lord says, "I will not blot his name out of the book of life." Those who are faithful to the Lord, those overcomers, have the promise of the Lord Himself that He will not blot their names out of the Book of Life but will confess them before His Father. Jesus demands that we confess Him before men and promises that if we do so He will confess us before His Father (Matt. 10:32). What a privilege! Have we ever stopped to think what it means to have our names presented before the God of the universe? Men consider it a great honor to be taken to Washington and introduced to the President of the United States, but that, by comparison, is nothing. To have our names presented before God is something to strive for, something to look forward to. May we be found faithful.

Each of these letters closes with a message to individuals. "He that hath an ear, let him hear what the Spirit saith unto the churches." It is possible to be orthodox and to be dead. It is possible to trust Christ and yet have no fruit in the life. Some today have a name that they live but are dead. Perhaps our friends think we are Christians. Perhaps our parents think we are a credit to them. Perhaps we attend church and maintain a good outward appearance. It is possible to have a name that we live but be dead. Let us search our hearts and ask whether we have real spiritual life or merely a name to live, whether we are fruitful in the service of Christ or as dead as the church at Sardis. Let us remember the words of the Lord and repent and dedicate ourselves anew to Him.

And shall I use these ransomed powers of mine
    For things that only minister to me?
Lord take my feet, my hands, my heart, my all
    And let me live and love and give for Thee.

PHILADELPHIA: A MISSIONARY CHURCH

Philadelphia is more obscure than most of the other seven cities of Revelation, for scant ruins remain to show us what the city was like. Founded about 140 B.C., Philadelphia was not an old city at the time John was writing. It was named after Attalus II, king of Pergamos, called Philadelphos ("brother lover") because of his love for and beneficent conduct toward his brother. Situated twenty-eight miles southeast of Sardis and about seventy-five miles from the coast on a great highway linking east and west, it stood on the border of Lydia, Phrygia, and Pisidia. Some think that Attalus founded the city at this location in order to represent Greek culture to the uncivilized regions beyond Lydia, to be a missionary to the barbarians. Whatever the reason, it did succeed in hellenizing the region, for by A.D. 19 the Lydian tongue had been superseded by the Greek.[22]

Philadelphia lay on the edge of a volcanic region known as the "burned land." Traces of volcanic eruptions remain in cinder heaps, hardened rivers of black lava, and steam geysers. The land was very fertile, and farming prospered. The city became the center of a

[22]Ramsay, p. 392.

great grape-growing area famous for its wines. Hot springs were common in the area and, indeed, still attract bathers for their medicinal properties. But this area was and even today is subject to violent earthquakes. The same quake that destroyed Sardis in A.D. 17 also devastated Philadelphia. For several years Philadelphia suffered lesser quakes almost daily. Three years after the great quake, according to the Greek geographer, Strabo, the people were still afraid; some lived in tents outside the city while others living within the city would rush out beyond the walls at every small shock to escape the danger of falling buildings.

The Roman emperor Tiberius helped to rebuild this city, as well as others, by remitting taxes and sending large sums of money. Philadelphia received the help with gratitude and not only erected a temple to the worship of the emperor but changed its name (with the emperor's permission) to Neacaesarea ("the new town of Caesar"). For some reason, however, the new name did not prove popular, and the city reverted to its old name after a few years.

The city had a custom concerning the beautiful temples dedicated to the many gods they worshiped. When a man served the city well as a citizen, performed some notable deed, or was known as a public benefactor and philanthropist, the city would erect, as a memorial to him, a column in one of the temples. All who came there to worship would see the name of this worthy man inscribed in the stone pillar.

After the capital of the Roman Empire shifted to Constantinople, Philadelphia's importance increased steadily. Favored in location, the city flourished in the trade that flowed from the east to the west. With the decline of the Byzantine Empire, it gained distinction as a strong outpost of Christianity. When the Muslim religion began to sweep over the western world, one by one the centers of Christianity fell before it. Prosperous, large Christian communities were completely destroyed by Muslim fanaticism. In Asia Minor, Philadelphia was the last Christian city to fall. Standing practically alone as a free Christian city in a Muslim land, Philadelphia twice overcame Turkish sieges. When it finally fell, it succumbed not to the might of the Turks alone but to the attack of a combined Turkish and Byzantine army. The Byzantine Christians, jealous of the success of Philadelphia, combined with the enemies of Christianity to destroy the city. It became a Muslim town and remains today as a small village called by the Turks, Alasehir. For centuries Philadelphia kept its character as a Christian city in the midst of a totally Muslim country. It kept the faith.

The Speaker to the Church

"To the angel of the church in Philadelphia write; These things saith he that is holy, he that is true, he that hath the key of David, he that openeth, and no man shutteth; and shutteth, and no man openeth" (Rev. 3:7). The Son, like the Father, is holy and true. If one is holy, he is also true. If one's character is right, if one is right inside, he will be true in his actions. It is said of the Lord that he has the key of David. Isaiah 22:22 mentions a treasurer of the temple named Shebna who apparently was unworthy of his office. Of him God says, "It shall come to pass in that day, I will call my servant Eliakim the son of Hilkiah: and I will clothe him with thy robe, and strengthen him with thy girdle, and I will commit thy government into his hand: and he shall be a father to the inhabitants of Jerusalem, and to the house of Judah. And the key of the house of David will I lay upon his shoulder; so he shall open and none shall shut; and he shall shut and none shall open." Notice that the key is to be laid on his shoulder. Keys evidently were different in those days from what they are now. Apparently doors were closed and locked by a wooden or iron bar dropped across the inside. The key must have been a piece of wood long enough to reach through a hole in the thick door to release the bar. This man, Eliakim, is a picture of the Lord Jesus Christ. He had the key of authority without which no one could enter the palace or the treasury. Eliakim opened and closed doors, and no one else could do anything about it. So it is that the Lord Jesus has the key of David. He has the authority. He opens and no man shuts. In the words of the song-writer, "He only can unlock the door of heaven and let us in."

The Opportunity of the Church

After saying, "I have the right to open, I have the right to close," our Lord tells this church, "I have set before thee an open door, and no man can shut it" (3:8). It is interesting that the Lord Jesus declares Himself to be the door: "I am the door of the sheep" (John 10:7-9). "He that entereth not by the door into the sheepfold, but climbeth up some other way, the same is a thief and a robber" (John 10:1). To the church at Philadelphia and to people today who are looking for forgiveness of sins, the Lord Jesus Christ is the only door of salvation.

But the door Christ mentions here is specifically a door of opportunity. That this meaning is intended is clear from Paul's use of the term in his epistles. On one occasion Paul, arriving at Troas, found that the Lord had opened to him a door of opportunity for service (II Cor. 2:12). On another occasion, writing from Ephesus, Paul requested prayer, saying, "A great door and effectual is opened unto me, and there are many adversaries" (I Cor. 16:8-9). He urges the Colossians to pray "that God would open unto us a door of utterance, to speak the mystery of Christ" (Col. 4:3). What the Lord is offering to this church is an opportunity for service and witness. The word "open" is not an adjective, as one might think from reading the English translation, but a perfect participle (*eneogmenen*) meaning "having been opened" or "standing open." At the time of the writing, God had opened the door, and it was standing open inviting men to enter.

The Lord is the One Who opens the door. It is vain for us to attempt to force our way through a door that He has not opened. But once He has opened the door, it is up to us to go through it. He does for us what we cannot do for ourselves, but we must respond with the ability that God has given us. As I write these words, I am convinced that the Lord has thrown open a door of service for many who read them. There are many open doors, many opportunities to serve the Lord today; but we must go through the doors, we must seize the opportunities. The Lord is not going to force anyone. For us, as for the Philadelphian church, a door is standing open to be entered.

Shortly after the Second World War, General Douglas MacArthur set up a provisional government in Japan to restore order. As he looked over the country and saw the receptivity of the people, he sent word back to the states requesting thousands of missionaries. The door was open, the opportunity golden. Japan welcomed the missionary. Its old religions had been undermined. The church, however, largely failed to enter that door, and Japan was lost to the gospel. When we see before us an open door, we should feel an obligation to enter it. Once after a service, a man approached Mr. Spurgeon and said, "Mr. Spurgeon, I have been listening to you preach for some time, and I have become interested in Christian work and feel that I ought to do something for the Lord; but I really don't know what to do. Could you suggest some way that I could be of service for the Lord?" Mr. Spurgeon asked, "What is your trade?" The man said, "I am an engineer on a train." Mr. Spurgeon replied, "You say that you are a Christian, that you really want to serve the Lord? What about your fireman who works with you, is he a Christian?" The man said, "I really don't know whether he is or not." Mr. Spurgeon then told him, "All right, the first thing you can do for the Lord is to go and find that fireman and see whether or not he is a Christian and lead him to Christ." A person is not going to be a good missionary in Japan or Africa or Brazil if he is not willing to serve the Lord here. Just going across the water does not make one a soulwinner. If one is not winning souls here, the Lord is not going to use him somewhere else. The opportunities are here for those willing to take them.

The Condition of the Church

Continuing to address the church, the Lord says, "Thou hast a little strength, and hast kept my word, and hast not denied my name" (3:8). God does not condemn a person merely for not being strong. He may condemn one who has little interest in His Word or in service, but he does not condemn one who has only a little strength so long as he uses that strength to the best of his ability. The church had kept God's Word and held on to His name. These two go together. One cannot deny the Bible and hold on to Jesus Christ. All we know of Christ we learn through His Word. Every word of the Bible is pure and true, and we cannot violate it or slight it and be true to Christ.

The church had maintained its strength, though small, in spite of persecution: "Behold, I will make them of the synagogue of Satan, which say they are Jews, and are not, but do lie; behold, I will make them to come and worship before thy feet, and to know that I have loved thee" (3:9). Its persecution, like that of the Smyrnan church, was by the "synagogue of Satan" (2:9; 3:9). The Jews, of all people, should worship Christ since Jesus came as their Messiah, but "He came unto his own, and his own received him not" (John 1:11). These Jews, having rejected Christ when He was presented to them, were really not Jews at all but a "synagogue of Satan." They were doing Satan's work, accomplishing his purpose under his control. In persecuting the church they were fulfilling the saying of Christ, "The time cometh, that whosoever killeth you will think that he doeth God service" (John 16:2).

We today have difficulty in realizing the tremendous pressure upon the early church. Alone in a hostile world, hated alike by Jews and pagans, pursued by the Roman government, threatened daily with loss of property or liberty or even life itself, ridiculed by neighbors and friends and family, boycotted and ostracized, the early Christians needed all the fortitude the grace of God could give to maintain their Christian witness without compromise. I wonder if we could stay true to Christ in such difficulties. Could we refuse to deny Him in the face of ridicule? Would we speak up for Christ when it was not popular or when our lives might be at stake? The severity of the persecution undergone by these Christians somewhat affected their outlook. Certain ones wrote descriptions of the hell that awaited their tormentors. Tertullian vividly described the agonies of the enemies of the church suffering God's judgment. He exulted in the fact that they were being made to suffer just as they had made the Christians suffer. Today we shrink back from it, but these early Christians had suffered so much that it is a wonder they did not hate their tormentors more than they did. Even Paul speaks of the time when Christ is going to return "in flaming fire taking vengeance on them that know not God" (II Thess. 1:8). These enemies of Philadelphia were to be vanquished. They would have to admit their defeat and their error as they acknowledged God's people. "Behold, I will make them to come and worship before thy feet, and to know that I have loved thee" (Rev. 3:9). How this promise was fulfilled in the history of the Philadelphian church we do not know. But the time is coming when every knee will bow and every tongue will confess that Christ is Lord (Phil. 2:10-11).

The Reward of the Church

The church was to be rewarded for staying true to Christ. "Because thou hast kept the word of my patience, saith the Lord, I also will keep thee from the hour of temptation [trial], which shall come upon all the world, to try them that dwell upon the earth" (3:10). We do not know from history just how this verse was fulfilled. Perhaps Philadelphia was spared from some wave of persecution that swept across the ancient world. We do know, however, that this promise will ultimately be fulfilled at the return of Christ. The day is coming when all of this world will experience trouble and calamity such as it has never known before. This tribulation—*the* great tribulation—will be caused not by wicked men but by God taking vengeance. During this period, God has promised to spare His people: "I also will keep thee from the hour of temptation [trial]" (3:10). God's judgments upon the unbelieving world will not fall upon his people. We look for the return of the Lord Jesus Christ, not for a time of tribulation.

The special message to individuals is, "Behold, I come quickly: hold that fast which thou hast, that no man take thy crown" (3:11). What did Philadelphia have? Not very much. Whereas Laodicea was a rich church, favored by men but condemned by God, Philadelphia was despised by men but praised by God. Philadelphia had only one thing: faithfulness. Both in John's day and in the centuries that followed, it stood fast. The last of the cities of Asia Minor to fall to the Turks, it fell not because of cowardice or negligence but through betrayal by compromising Christian cities jealous of its honor. Knowing its faithfulness, present and future, Jesus says, Let "no man take thy crown." We need not think of literal crowns exclusively, although they may be included. A crown is a reward. Whereas the overcomers at Smyrna were promised a crown of life, of these at Philadelphia He says, "Him that overcometh will I make a pillar in the temple of my God" (3:12). This promise may refer to the custom of carving the name of a prominent citizen on a pillar in one of the city's temples. The reward promised by the Lord is not a memorial inscribed on a pillar in an earthly temple, of which Philadelphia—"little Athens" —had so many, but being made "a pillar in the temple of my God," that is, in heaven.

The Lord promises something else: "He shall go no more out" (3:12). It was mentioned earlier that Philadelphia was in a region of earthquakes. Long after the tremendous quake that destroyed the city in A.D. 17, Philadelphia had lesser quakes almost daily. Three years after the earthquake, Strabo wrote: "In Philadelphia ... not even the walls are safe, but in a sense are shaken and caused to crack every day. And the inhabitants are continually attentive to the disturbance in the earth and plan all their structures with a view to their occurrence.... Incessantly the walls of the houses are cracked, different parts of the city being thus affected at different times. For this reason but few people live in the city, and most of them spend their lives as farmers in the country" (*Geography*, 12. 8. 18; 13. 4. 10). In 1973 an earthquake struck this same region, and the newspapers reported that the people rushed out of their houses to avoid falling walls. This was the way the Philadelphians lived for years. It was to these people that the Lord promises, "You will no more go out." The overcomers will forever be secure in God's house with Him.

> I'll exchange my cross for a starry crown
> > Where the gates swing outward never.
> At His feet I'll lay every burden down
> > And with Jesus reign forever.

Lastly, the Lord says, "I will write upon him the name of my God, and the name of the city of my God, which is new Jerusalem, which cometh down out of heaven from my God: and I will write upon him my new name" (3:12).

When Tiberius helped the city rebuild after the great earthquake, the grateful citizens changed the name of their city from Philadelphia to "New Caesar." Accordingly, God says that He will give them another name, "the name of my God, and the name of the city of my God, which is new Jerusalem" (3:12). Whereas the city, a generation later, resumed its earlier name, the new name bestowed by God will be an eternal memorial.

Both Philadelphia, the city, and Philadelphia, the church, were missionary from their outset. The church had a wonderful opportunity to preach the gospel and stand for the Lord Jesus Christ—the opportunity of a door standing open. That the church entered the door of opportunity is not stated but rather implied in the divine commendation. Like the Philadelphians, each of us faces an open door this day. God opens the door, but we must enter it. Is it the door of salvation? The door of service? Have you told the Lord, "I will be willing to do whatever You want me to do?" A door of service for the Lord may seem insignificant. But if we are faithful in doing what the Lord gives us to do, He will open another door of greater responsibility. God needs workers today just as in the first century. Surely He is not going to refuse to use a person who wants to serve Him. The harvest is white. The fields are ready. People need Christ. The opportunity is before us. Are we going to enter the door of opportunity or neglect it? Let no man take thy crown. The Christian life is a struggle, a conflict. I am convinced that no one can forcibly take our reward from us. Only we, by our indifference and neglect, can let it go. If we refuse to enter the door that He opens for us, God's work will get done but we will lose our crown.

> Fight the good fight with all thy might!
> Christ is thy strength, and Christ thy right;
> Lay hold on life and it shall be
> Thy joy and crown eternally.

LAODICEA: A COMPLACENT CHURCH

About a hundred miles from the Aegean coast of Turkey and forty miles southeast of Philadelphia and almost due east of Ephesus lie the three cities of Colosse, Hieropolis, and Laodicea, only a few miles apart in the valley of the Lycus River. Paul wrote a letter to the church at Colosse and one to Philemon, who probably lived there. Nothing has been done systematically to excavate Colosse, and almost nothing is known about it today. In the Colossian letter Paul refers briefly to Hieropolis (Col. 4:13). Numerous ruins from this city have been brought to light including a very extensive necropolis (cemetery) and a large theater. Papias, one of the early Christian writers, was pastor here when John wrote the Book of Revelation.

In the Colossian letter, several references by Paul to Laodicea probably indicate that he knew some Christians there and had visited there. Since the city lay on one of the main trade routes to the Aegean coast, Paul could easily have passed through it on one of his journeys. At any rate, he shows his intense concern for this church, as well as for the Colossian church, when he says, "For I would that ye knew what great conflict I have for you, and for them at Laodicea, and for as many as have not seen my face in the flesh" (Col. 2:1).

He says of Epaphras, "For I bear him record, that he hath a great zeal for you, and them that are in Laodicea, and them in Hieropolis" (4:13). Epaphras may have been the one who first brought the gospel to Laodicea. In closing his letter Paul says, "Salute the brethren which are in Laodicea, and Nymphas, and the church which is in his house" (4:15) and mentions a letter to the Laodiceans that is to be exchanged with theirs (4:16). These three churches were as closely related as the three cities, not just geographically but in the bonds of Christian fellowship.

Laodicea was founded by Antiochus II about 250 B.C. and named after his wife. Being built at the point where the Lycus River valley joins that of the Maeander, it had three important roads passing through or near it. One ran from the Mediterranean coastal towns of Perga and Attalia (Perge and Antalya) and could have been used by Paul as he traveled between Antioch and Attalia on his first journey. Another came from Sardis and Philadelphia, and a third from the northeastern region of Phrygia and central Turkey. Over the years the passage of trade along these roads made the city into a great commercial center. The city had an active wool industry; its farmers raised a breed of black sheep famous for the softness and beauty of their wool. It also manufactured a powder or tablet called collyrium, used in treating eye ailments. The word used by John and translated "eyesalve" is the same that the physician Galen used to describe a Phrygian preparation to strengthen weak eyes. As a consequence of its material prosperity, Laodicea attained fame as a banking center. When Cicero was traveling in the east (about a hundred years before Paul's first journey), he cashed his letters of credit in Laodicea and spent several months there.

In A.D. 17 the city was destroyed by the great earthquake, previously mentioned, that devastated the entire region. Along with other cities it was rebuilt with

help from the Roman emperor Tiberius. When it was
again destroyed in A.D. 60, the citizens of the city
refused all help from the Roman government and
rebuilt the city at their own expense. Tacitus, the
Roman historian, said, "Laodicea arose from the ruins
by the strength of her own resources and with no help
from us."

In 133 B.C. the city became part of the Roman
Empire when the king of Pergamos willed his kingdom
to Rome. Rome established at Laodicea a circuit court,
from which justice was administered to the surrounding district. Large numbers of Jews lived there. Free
citizenship was offered any Jews who would settle
there, because they made good, useful citizens and
were skilled craftsmen. Their number may be judged
from the following facts. In A.D. 62, Flaccus, governor
of Asia, issued a decree forbidding the export of gold.
The Jews had a custom of sending each year to Jerusalem the temple tax of half a shekel and usually
sent it as a bulk shipment in gold. They ignored the
ban and sent the gold as usual. The Roman authorities,
learning of the shipment, confiscated it. When weighed,
it came to twenty pounds or fifteen thousand drachmas. Since a half shekel is two drachmas, approxi-
mately seventy-five hundred Jews lived in Laodicea
and its vicinity and joined in making the contribution.
These Jews were so powerful in the city that they could
influence the Roman government to permit them to
observe their Sabbath laws and other customs even
over the objection of some of the local officials.

Although it had no high mountain nearby as had
Pergamos and Sardis, Laodicea was a strong city. It
guarded the trade route that passed right through the
center of the city. Its main weakness was that it had
no source of good water nearby. Water was brought
into the city from several miles away by aqueduct. An
attacking force had only to cut off the water supply
at a safe distance from the city in order to force the

inhabitants into an impossible position; they could not withstand a long siege. This realization led the Laodiceans to become diplomats rather than warriors. They succeeded in reaching agreements with many of their enemies and lived in peace even before the enforced peace of the Romans. Spared from the ravages of war, they became immensely wealthy and lived in confidence and security, needing nothing.

In 129 B.C. Laodicea became part of the province of Asia. Mark Anthony conferred Roman citizenship on its citizens in return for their defense against a Parthian attack. They worshiped Zeus, the main god in their religion, along with the Anatolian moon god, Men; some lesser gods; and, of course, the emperor. Toward the end of the second century of this era, the city received the coveted title of *Neokoros,* temple keeper. With the triumph of Christianity, it became the seat of a bishopric. An ecumenical council was held there in the fourth century.

Another earthquake struck the city and destroyed it in A.D. 494. It never recovered from this blow and continued only as a small village until the Turkish conquest of the fifteenth century. The city we see today dates entirely from the Roman period, including ruins of two theaters and a stadium dedicated to Vespasian in A.D. 79. There also remain portions of walls with two gates, one dedicated to Domitian, the emperor who ruled when John wrote the Revelation. On the east is the Syrian gate; on the west, the Ephesian gate. Remains of the aqueduct may be seen. Fed from a spring near the modern city of Denezli, it ran for five miles and dropped 350 feet. Carrying water heavy with lime, the pipes were often stopped up by sediment.

Like the other churches to which John wrote, the church of Laodicea reflected the condition of the city. This church was not guilty of immorality, false teaching, or strife. Its sin was complacency, lukewarmness. Some have suggested that the angel of the church was Archippus, mentioned by Paul as being in Colosse (Philem. 2). In the rather late *Apostolic Constitutions* (viii. 46) he is said to have been the first bishop of Laodicea. In Colossians 4:17 Paul exhorts him to take heed to his ministry. It is possible that he is the one who is rebuked by the Lord in this letter.

Christ describes Himself to this church as "the Amen, the faithful and true witness, the beginning of the creation of God" (Rev. 3:14). These are terms with a solemn and majestic ring to them. Amen means "so be it." Seiss says, "It is not an oath, yet it has much of the solemnity and force of an oath. It contains no adjuration or appeal, yet it authenticates, confirms, binds, seals, and pledges to the truth of that to which it is affixed" (p. 245). Christ is picturing Himself as the confirmer of all truth; but, more than that, He *is* the truth (John 14:6). As the "faithful and true witness," He testifies to the truth of God. He makes known to us the will of God for our salvation and growth in grace. "We speak that we do know, and testify that we have seen" (John 3:11). His testimony is always true.

The phrase "the beginning of the creation of God" has been construed by some as teaching that Christ was a created being rather than the Lord of the universe. But the word translated "beginning" (*arche*) in this verse means not "beginning" in the sense of the first part or phase but "source" or "origin." Christ is not a part of creation, not that which God created first, but the source, the fountainhead of creation. "All things were made by him; and without him was not anything made that was made" (John 1:3; see also John 5:19; I Cor. 8:6; Heb. 1:2-3; and Rev. 1:17). In the letter to Colosse that was read by the Laodicean church, Paul makes the matter perfectly clear by referring to Christ as the one "who is the image of the invisible God, the firstborn of every creature" and explaining "for by him were all things created, that are in heaven, and that are in earth, visible and invisible, whether they be thrones, or dominions, or principalities, or powers: all things were created by him, and for him: and he is before all things, and by him all things consist" (1:15-17). To Laodicea, lifeless and indifferent and cool, the Lord speaks as the One who is the source of all life, the infinite energy, the origin and means of God's creation.

The Condition of the Church

"I know thy works, that thou art neither cold nor hot: I would thou wert cold or hot. So then because thou art lukewarm, and neither cold nor hot, I will spue thee out of my mouth" (3:15-16). As one stands today on the ruins of an ancient church amidst the ruins of Laodicea, he can see in the distance the white cliffs of Hieropolis produced by the chalky white deposit of the mineral springs that flow over the brink into the valley—a striking formation called by the modern Turks *Pamukkale,* or cotton palace. These springs were famous in antiquity and are often visited today for their therapeutic qualities. The waters are very warm (almost ninety degrees), brackish, and nauseous to the taste. When the Lord referred to the Laodiceans as "neither cold nor hot" and destined to be spewed out, they would naturally have thought of these hot bubbling springs nearby.

Lukewarmness is a transitional state. Water is lukewarm before becoming cold or hot. Usually, however, the lukewarm stage is passed swiftly. It is lukewarmness as a static condition that the Lord deplores. Of the seven cities Laodicea is the one that is the least determined in character, the least clearly outlined in history. Its chief characteristic was adaptability. Likewise, the Laodicean church remained lukewarm. Unable to reject the allurements of the world, it would be rejected absolutely and inexorably by Him whose faithfulness and truth reject all half-heartedness and compromise.

No sense of need. Spiritually speaking, to be luke-warm is to be indifferent and complacent toward one's need. Laodicea was a wealthy city, and the church prospered with the city. Materially "rich, and increased with goods" (3:17), the church thought itself well off in grace also. It had "need of nothing." Its blindness was that of the welfare state today. Better pay, better housing, better education—these, it is said, will solve our problems. Strangely enough, new-evangelicals are joining the liberals in crying out for social improvement; their evangelism consists not in proclaiming the message of salvation through faith in the work of Christ but in providing material benefits. Stress on the material, on numbers, on size, with neglect of the spiritual—what a picture of the church today! This bubble of false prosperity bursts with the Lord's assessment of such a church as "wretched, and miserable, and poor, and blind and naked" (3:17). The wealthy Laodiceans were poor! Manufacturers of eye salve were blind! Producers of beautiful woolen garments were naked! The Laodiceans were a mistaken, deceived church. Trusting in material prosperity to commend them to God, they forgot the lesson of the rich man and Lazarus (Luke 16) and the parable of the rich fool (Luke 12).

They trusted in material things because they were lukewarm. The cold are easier to reach than the luke-warm. The publicans and harlots were spiritually cold, but they listened to Christ. The scribes and Pharisees were lukewarm—too religious, too set in their ways, too complacent, to face their true condition and repent. Jesus said to them, "The publicans and the harlots go into the kingdom of God before you" (Matt. 21:31). If they had been cold, without the outward forms of religion and with no profession of godliness, they would not have presumed to have confidence in God's favor. Had they been hot, they would have had the spiritual discernment to see that the things of this world are temporal and pass away. But, alas, their lukewarmness made them lazy and dull and indifferent to self-examination. They falsely concluded that they were all God expected them to be. Such self-deception is present in churches and in Christians today. We have just enough Christianity to ease our conscience and still our fears of judgment but not enough to keep us dissatisfied with ourselves and seeking to grow in the Christian life.

One problem of this church was that it had no persecution. There was no opposition from the Jews, no trouble from the advocates of emperor worship, no difficulty from the Roman officials. The Laodiceans, having no challenge to their faith, were not forced to seek God and depend on Him. They felt self-sufficient. Smyrna needed encouragement and help, Pergamos was located in Satan's stronghold, but Laodicea had need of nothing. It cannot be without significance that the two churches about whom nothing bad is said (Smyrna and Philadelphia) were both engaged in a struggle for their existence, whereas the two churches that seem to have been in the worst condition spiritually (Sardis and Laodicea) were at rest. No sooner did the emperor Constantine profess conversion and make Christianity a religion protected and promoted by the state than the church went into a rapid decline morally, spiritually, and doctrinally. When Christianity won its battle with the Roman Empire, it lost its war with the world and the devil. It lost its pilgrim character, its separation from sin and worldliness, and its spiritual power to transform lives. Persecution of the church is not entirely a curse, and for the church on earth, rest is not an unmixed blessing.

The Christians at Laodicea saw no need to improve their lives. They were perfectly satisfied. We sing, "Just as I Am" and "Come Just as You Are," hymns that present the great truth that God will save us out of our sin without any reformation or preparatory good works on our part. But God does not expect us to *stay* "just as we are." He wants us to grow in grace and holiness. "This is the will of God, even your sanctification" (I Thess. 4:3).

Centuries before, the prophet Ezekiel, writing from Babylon to a sinful, indifferent, and apostate Judah, had said, "Behold, this was the iniquity of thy sister Sodom, pride, fulness of bread, and abundance of idleness was in her" (Ezek. 16:49). What a prophetic description of Laodicea! What a startling description of America today! Does not our wickedness, lawlessness, and moral decay stem from these very three things?

No enthusiasm. Lack of enthusiasm is the essence of lukewarmness. There can be no real religion without enthusiasm. The phrase "lukewarm Christian" is really a contradiction in terms. The Laodicean church was neither very much for nor very much against anything. It was completely blase. Nothing excited it. Have you ever gotten a dead-fish or dishrag handshake? If any shaking is to be done, you must do it for the other person too. Such describes the church of Laodicea—listless and useless. In Corinth, Paul was brought before the Roman magistrate, Gallio, who refused to hear the case. A riot ensued, and the ruler of the synagogue was beaten before the judgment seat. Luke's comment was "and Gallio cared for none of those things" (Acts 18:17). A Roman official, responsible to administer justice, was indifferent to what was going on before his eyes. This indifference characterized the Laodiceans. They could not have cared less. The challenge was gone and with it the enthusiasm necessary to accomplish anything for God.

No vision. The church, the Lord says, is blind. The sellers of eye salve should anoint their own eyes that they might see. Of the Pharisees Jesus had said, "If ye were blind, ye should have no sin: but now ye say, we see; therefore your sin remaineth" (John 9:41). If they had been willing to admit their blindness, there would have been hope for them, but they would not. To the end they affirmed "we see." Similarly, the Laodiceans did not even realize they were blind. They were to "buy gold," not from merchants but from Christ and not with their abundance of money but with suffering, fidelity to truth, and perhaps martyrdom. "Where there is no vision, the people perish, " said the writer of Proverbs (29:18). Laodicea was blind to its spiritual need and ready to perish. They must also have been blind to the need of others. Many Jews lived in and around the city, and if the church had been winning some of these to Christ, the rest would have been opposing the church just as they opposed Paul years earlier. They came to church and enjoyed the fellowship but made no effort to reach the lost. Many churches and individuals today are in this condition. All interest in the Lord's work is gone; all sense of need has long been lost; vision, if there ever was any, has faded, and blindness has set in. The rest of the letter holds out hope for escape from this dreadful condition.

The Choice of the Church

As in the case of Pergamos, a distinction must be made between the church corporately and its members individually. The church at Laodicea was about to be totally rejected. "I will spue thee out of my mouth" (3:16). To the individual members, however, the Lord offers a choice. Sad as conditions were, the time was not, for the individual, too late. He must repent or face retribution.

Repentance. "As many as I love, I rebuke and chasten: be zealous therefore, and repent" (3:19). Christ here uses the same word for love (*phileo*) that he used when He asked Peter, "Lovest thou me?" (John 21:17). It signifies a more personal, tender relationship than *agapao* and is usually used of the love of family and friends. Although the Christians in this church were poor in spiritual matters and lacked enthusiasm for the things of God, the Lord still loved them. "God commendeth his love toward us, in that, while we were yet sinners, Christ died for us" (Rom. 5:8). As God loved us in our sin before saving us, so He loves us after we become His people, imperfect though we be. Nothing can separate us from the love of Christ, exclaims Paul (Rom. 8:35-39). But because He loves, He rebukes and chastens. The stinging rebuke administered to this church was a token of God's love for them. "Open rebuke is better than secret love," said Solomon (Prov. 27:5). Love does not keep silent in the presence of sin, but rebukes it.

Love also brings chastisement. The writer of Hebrews says that God "scourgeth every son whom he receiveth" (Heb. 12:6) and that chastisement is a sign of sonship. Any father who refuses to chasten his son is negligent in his duty. Chastisement is not only punishment but discipline. It is designed to teach: to correct and improve the person punished. As a means of instruction, it is not pleasant but necessary and, to those who heed it, of great profit. If Christ had not loved this church, He would simply have left it alone. If God ever abandons a man, his condition is sad indeed. This is the danger warned against by the writer of Hebrews (6:4-8; 10:26-31). The only way to be excepted from discipline is to be excepted from sonship.

"Be zealous therefore, and repent" (Rev. 3:9). Repentance involves, first of all, a change of mind or attitude from unconcern to sorrow for past failures. It involves, secondly, a change of conduct. The church must change its ways: it must get true wealth from Christ— gold that will not perish. It must forget its luxurious clothing, purchased from the many shops and caravans of the city, and buy from Christ white raiment, typifying the righteousness given by Christ, to cover its nakedness. It must use eye salve supplied by Christ to gain spiritual sight. The words "be zealous" and "repent," in reference to separate actions, are in emphatic, not chronological, order; and for the sake of analysis the order may be reversed. "Repent," in the original, is an aorist imperative, which stresses a simple action taking place at some point of time. "Be zealous" is a present imperative, which refers not to a single act but to a continual process or a series of actions. By means of these verb forms, the Lord is saying that the church must (1) come to a time, a specific moment, when it faces the facts about itself— realizes its guilt and failure—and changes its attitude and direction once for all (repentance) and (2) demonstrate this change in a new course of action, which consists in living continuously in harmony with the will of God (zeal). Repentance and zeal go together. One is no good without the other. Zeal without repentance only leads further astray; repentance without zeal falls short of true repentance unto life.

The Laodicean church had everything except Christ. He had been excluded from the church. Hence the invitation, "Behold, I stand at the door, and knock: if any man hear my voice, and open the door, I will come in to him, and will sup with him, and he with me" (3:20). John said in his Gospel, "He came unto his own, and his own received him not" (1:11). We marvel that the world could resist the appeal of Christ on earth. But now we see the risen, ascended Lord rejected by His own church. Those who call themselves by His name and who represent themselves to the world as His church have rejected Him and excluded Him from their midst. The Lord stands outside the assembly knocking for admission. At Christ's return, the professing church as a whole will be apostate and will not receive Him.

This knocking may be interpreted in several ways, each with elements of Biblical truth. First, the Lord was standing outside the door of the Laodicean church, pleading for admittance. The only cure for their lukewarmness was to readmit the excluded Christ.

Second, the knocking has often been interpreted as Christ standing and knocking at the door of the heart of the individual sinner of all ages with the gospel invitation. This application is appropriate, for Christ first comes to us, not we to Christ. "He at whose door we ought to stand, for He *is* the door (John 10:7), who, as such, has bidden *us* to knock (Matt. 7:7; Luke 11:9), is content that the whole relation between Him and us be reversed."[23] Christ will not force an entry. We must open the door. The famous painting by Solman portrays the Lord standing with raised hand knocking on a door that has no outside latch. Although the Spirit helps our natural weakness in persuading and enabling us to respond (Luke writes of Lydia, "Whose heart the Lord opened," Acts 16:14), each of us must unlatch the door from within. It is God's work, but it is also man's responsibility. Man can open only when Christ knocks, but man must open.

On being permitted to enter, Christ entertains His host. "Receiving Him to sup with us at our earthly tables, He proposes to have us sup with Him at His heavenly banquet."[24] Of the three meals usually eaten in New Testament times, supper was the most important. Breakfast was light, and lunch or dinner was usually eaten hurriedly before work resumed. At the end of the day, after work was done and put aside, the family ate together its main meal. Supper (*deipnion*) was a time for relaxation and fellowship. This is what Christ offers to those who permit him to enter.

[23]Trench, p. 223.

[24]J.A. Seiss, *Letters to the Seven Churches* (Grand Rapids: Baker, 1956), p. 314.

Third, since Revelation is a book of the second coming of Christ, this requested entrance may have some special reference to His return. Such is the meaning of Christ's coming in the other letters. To Pergamos, He says, "I will come unto thee quickly, and will fight against them with the sword of my mouth" (2:16; cf. 19:15); to Thyatira, "Hold fast till I come" (2:25); to Sardis, "I will come on thee as a thief, and thou shalt not know what hour I will come upon thee" (3:3); to Philadelphia, "Behold, I come quickly" (3:11). While on earth, our Lord warned: "Let your loins be girded about, and your lamps burning; and ye yourselves like unto men that wait for their lord, when he will return from the wedding; that when he cometh and knocketh, they may open unto him immediately. Blessed are those servants, whom the lord when he cometh shall find watching: verily I say unto you, that he shall gird himself, and make them to sit down to meat, and will come forth and serve them. And if he shall come in the second watch, or come in the third watch, and find them so, blessed are those servants" (Luke 12:35-38). Here in this incident are the same coming, the same knocking, and the same supping with those who open that appear in the message to Laodicea. If Laodicea is, as some think, a picture of the church of the last days before the return of Christ, then this knocking may be some special annunciation of the presence of the Saviour at the point of His returning—one last special appeal before it becomes too late and man's destiny is unalterably fixed.

Judgment. The alternative to repentance and admittance of Christ is judgment. The return of Christ is the "blessed hope" (Titus 2:13) to those who have heard the knock of the Saviour and opened to Him. But His coming will bring judgment upon those who know Him not. There is a judgment of words (Matt. 12:36), deeds (Rev. 20:12), and neglect of duty (Matt. 25:27). Christ will return "in flaming fire taking vengeance on them that know not God, and that obey not the gospel of our Lord Jesus Christ" (II Thess. 1:8).

This judgment may be averted by the concerned sinner. The Lord judged our sin as He hung on the cross, bearing our guilt and penalty. Those who hear His knock and open to Him in faith and repentance can say in triumph with Paul, "There is therefore now no condemnation to them which are in Christ Jesus" (Rom. 8:1).

> Bold shall I stand in that great day;
>> For who ought to my charge shall lay.
> Fully absolved from these I am;
>> From sin and fear, from guilt and shame.

With the warning and the invitation is a promise of reward: "To him that overcometh will I grant to sit with me in my throne, even as I also overcame, and am set down with my Father in his throne" (3:21). When Christ was on earth, He told the disciples they would sit on twelve thrones judging the twelve tribes of Israel (Matt. 19:28). When James and John asked to sit on His right and left hand, He did not deny that these were places of honor in the kingdom but said that they would be assigned by the Father (Matt. 20:23). Paul said, "If we suffer [with Him], we shall also reign with him" (II Tim. 2:12). He asked the Corinthians, "Do ye not know that the saints shall judge the world? Know ye not that we shall judge angels?" (I Cor. 6:2-3). It is abundantly clear in the New Testament that the saints will reign with Christ when He returns to earth and establishes His kingdom. Two thrones are mentioned. Since Christ came to earth and suffered the opposition of the world and the devil and overcame them, He has been sitting on the Father's throne. He is waiting for the day when He will set up His kingdom on earth, at which time His enemies will become the footstool of

His feet and He will sit upon His own throne.

This promise of reigning with Christ is for over-comers only. Not every member of the Laodicean church could claim it. Professing the name of Christ and having one's name on the roll of a church is not enough. There was much in this church to deter its members from finding a true, living relationship with Christ. Many who started out had fallen by the way-side, been choked by thorns of worldliness, or wilted in the heat of opposition. Those who survived these obstacles, who overcame, would be rewarded by shar-ing with their Lord the glories and pleasures of His kingdom. Christ had overcome these difficulties and could provide victory, just as He can for His people today.

This letter and this section of the Book of Revelation close with the usual exhortation for those who hear to heed the message. How many today hear the message of salvation but heed it not! How many know the truth but do not avail themselves of it! May God open the ears and stir the hearts of some who read these mes-sages from the first century and move them to faith in the Saviour, dedication to His cause, and determina-tion to stand in the midst of persecution, opposing all that is false in the church today.